ON THE EDGE OF THE

ON THE EDGE OF THE WORLD

by
NIKOLAI LESKOV

Translated from the Russian with notes
by
MICHAEL PROKURAT

Illustrated by
TATIANA MISIJUK

ST. VLADIMIR'S SEMINARY PRESS
Crestwood, NY 10707
1992

Library of Congress Cataloging-in-Publication Data

Leskov, N. S. (Nikolai Semenovich), 1831-1895.
   [Na kraiu sveta. English]
   On the edge of the world / by Nikolai Leskov ; translated from the Russian with notes by
Michael Prokurat.
    p.   cm.
   Includes bibliographical references.
   ISBN 0–88141–118–3
   I. Title.
PG3337.L5R9213   1992
891.73'3—dc20

                          92–31940
                             CIP

ON THE EDGE OF THE WORLD

English language translation
Copyright © 1992

by

ST VLADIMIR'S SEMINARY PRESS

ISBN 0–88141–118–3

PRINTED IN THE UNITED STATES OF AMERICA

Contents

Translator's Preface

Nikolai S. Leskov (1831-1895) wrote and rewrote *On the Edge of the World* until it took its present, final shape in late 1875 and 1876. Neither the novel nor the author won critical acclaim, although a wide readership liked both. In fact, Leskov's reputation was acknowledged only rarely during his lifetime; but it grew in Russia (and in Germany) after his death, due to a new edition of his works in 1902-3, a few positive critical books, and some new literary disciples. *On the Edge of the World* (hereafter *On the Edge*) was somewhat dangerous. It criticized the church using the church's own theology, and challenged views of government and religion which were widespread in Europe.

Leskov was not a member of the aristocracy nor of the intelligentsia, both supposed requirements for literati in Russia. He dropped out of school early in life, without even completing the gymnasium, and later became a traveling government employee and a businessman. When he began writing professionally at age thirty he considered himself a journalist—but quickly transformed these same journalistic skills into tools for the art of the short story, much as Tolstoy transformed his skills as a diarist. Thus, Leskov wrote no juvenilia but emerged as a mature, developed writer. Still, he never mastered the "great form" of his time, the long novel; and it was probably a combination of these factors which deprived him of the recognition from his contemporaries he deserved. After he established his professional reputation, Leskov often felt cheated out of his rightful glory and continually battled feelings of inadequacy.

The characteristics which marred Leskov's artistic reputation during his lifetime—no formal education, ex-itinerant employee, writer of the shorter forms, etc.—were the very features of his artistic genius. They gave him his identity, his self-image

7

as the man of experience, the man well-traveled on the byroads of the most unfamiliar of the Russian provinces. Resultingly, Leskov chose the travelogue, as in this novel, to be one of his favorite genres. In the travelogue or travel diary, as in other of his journalistic modes, the contents were usually half fact and half fiction, though this remained indiscernible to the reader. Hugh McLean, the international dean of Leskov studies, has described this type of writing as "ambiguous fictionality: dancing continually on the very border separating reality from art."

Leskov's out-of-the-way peregrinations and his peculiarly acute ear for language enabled him to portray characters in dialect, just as revolutionary a concept in Russia as in America for his contemporary, Mark Twain. Both Leskov and Twain enjoy many other similarities: beginnings in itinerant work and then in journalism, devotion to narration or basic storytelling, mastery of style, thematic utilization of travel, extensive use of the tongue in cheek manner, personal interest in religion, usage of spoken—as opposed to literary—language, etc. Unlike Twain, Leskov created characters in dialect solely through "mannered" language and "the pitching of the voice," not with the added tools of defective spelling and mispronunciation which Twain so successfully employed. Leskov did this primarily through the selection of vocabulary. Leskov's stylized vocabulary alone fostered the individualization of speech, giving the impression of words spoken, of oralization. McLean tells us, "In matters of Russian vocabulary he was perhaps the greatest connoisseur of all the foremost Russian writers, the one most at home in unfrequented byways of regional and class dialects, the most inventive linguistic innovator."

Leskov's linguistic innovation (a nightmare for translators) was seldom appreciated by his conservative literary colleagues. First of all, from time to time he used what experts term "macaronics" and "blend-words," or what might more familiarly be called "nonexistent words" (*slovechki*) or "unwords." He sparked a continuing debate in Russia on the legitimacy of his invention and on his sense of proportion. (As an illustration of the literary difficulty at issue, it is notable that writers like Lewis Carroll or Gerard Manley Hopkins were not known in nineteenth-century Russia.) Second, Leskov employed folk etymologies to "redefine" words and give them peculiar new definitions, a type of neologism. Although his use of this device in *On the Edge* is limited, one may consult the Book of Genesis which is replete with Hebrew folk etymologies[1] for more examples of the phenomenon. This too did not endear him to literary purists—but it makes him fun to read!

After the completion of *Cathedral Folk* (1872), a masterful portrayal of Russian parish clergy, Leskov was considered the leading writer on, and defender of, Orthodoxy. Authorship of *On the Edge* reinforced this view. The type of "defender of Orthodoxy" that Leskov was for the first part of his literary career should be examined, since the nuances are appreciable. Leskov was champion of the parish priest, a priest as he imagined his paternal grandfather to be, kind to his flock and steadfast before the arbitrary decisions of civil and ecclesiastical authorities. If champion of the parish clergy, he was equally the declared foe of the bishops and church-state officialdom. His dislike of the hierarchy, the Holy Synod, and the Ober-Procurator remained relatively undisguised. However, his knowledge of theology, theological literature, and liturgy was formidable. Many of the materials he selected from church tradition to publish were recommended readings by parish clergy to their flocks, and occasionally were even republished by the church. Some of this publication activity occurred late in his career. Thus, the title won early in his career, "defender of Orthodoxy," is to be qualified and understood with some reservations.

In a brief analysis of Leskov's attitude toward Christianity, it should be pointed out that during this period in his life Roman Catholicism and Protestantism do not seem to have fared any better, or worse, than Orthodoxy. Shortly after writing *On the Edge* on a trip to Paris—the most significant feature of which was a long, cordial stay and dialogue with Russian Jesuits there—Leskov expressed sympathy with Jesuit ideas and ministry. Still, he did not shy away from roundly criticizing certain Roman doctrinal positions he considered recent and innovative,

1 E.g., "No longer shall your name be Abram ('exalted ancestor'), but your name shall be Abraham (here, understood as 'ancestor of a multitude')." In point of fact the name Abraham is a dialectical variant of Abram.

as well as the tendency of the Roman Church to provide sure answers where there are none, to paraphrase his complaint.

His attitude toward Radstockism (discussed in the Notes) and Protestantism bear similar marks of praise and scepticism. One might have expected more sympathy from Leskov toward Lord Radstock (comparable in spirit to Billy Graham) in Russia. The evangelical Englishman did not speak against any denomination, but characterized organized religion as dominated by a formalism that eclipsed the essence and true spirit of the Christian faith—notes that Leskov himself would play. However, in 1876 he published a treatise which became a book the next year, *A High-Society Schism: Lord Radstock, His Doctrine and Preaching*. In this Leskov asked whether Radstock had not erred in his personal judgment by claiming too much authority for his own rationale and faith. Edmund Heier comments:

> Leskov's criticism touches the very essence of Radstockism, and with it also the entire Protestant doctrine of justification by faith. He argues against the concept of salvation by faith and redemption through the atoning death of Jesus Christ. Against any passage which Lord Radstock cites from the Bible in defence of his teaching, others may be selected which express the very opposite.[2]

As the scholar W. B. Edgerton and others have observed, Leskov took to task anyone who dogmatically claimed "he [had] found the one correct path to the truth." He was capable of positively appreciating any belief that promoted practical Christianity, "true Christianity"—but denominational exclusivity expressed by any religious group brought his wrath. This might explain his dual attitude, praise and condemnation, toward every Christian church body. It was not entirely a doctrinal or ecclesiastical position, but possibly a reflection of his own search for religious truth.

By the 1870s and to the end of his life, Leskov both exhibited a knowledge of the tenets of Protestantism and evolved into a Tolstoyan of sorts, although he was never officially excommunicated as was his idol, Tolstoy. Given his "transvaluation of

2 Edmund Heier, *Religious Schism in the Russian Aristocracy 1860-1900: Radstockism and Pashkovism* (The Hague: Martinus Nijhoff, 1970), p. 69.

faith," one goal of scholarship has been to plot the course of this evolutionary journey in his life and writings. Sorting out the dynamics of that process is far beyond the scope of this preface, but whereas Leskov began as a "defender of Orthodoxy" and that he ended up as a modified Tolstoyan are beyond dispute. Briefly put, depending on how one views Leskov's development, *On the Edge* may be attributed to his "Orthodox period," his "Protestant leanings," or to his "abandonment of Orthodoxy." Unfortunately, this type of analysis—as logical and necessary as it is—runs the risk of overlooking what might be the most important aspect of Leskov's legitimate understanding of Orthodox Christianity.

The point glossed over is that Leskov used traditional (or Traditional in the Orthodox Christian sense), ancient ecclesiastical authorities to express views on what should be done by Christians, and to oppose Christianity improperly practiced in Russia. When this was subterfuge to avoid censorship or diminution of his social position is extremely difficult to discern, since the positions taken were not merely contentious, but were by and large expert argumentations, correct according to Holy Tradition. When Leskov through the mouth of the archbishop opposed modern novelty in religious painting, he appealed to the traditional canon of classical iconography. When through the words of Kiriak he criticized baptism without preparation and catechesis, he quoted Saint Cyril of Jerusalem on the sacrament of baptism. When again, through Kiriak, he critiqued the minimalistic morality of Christian urban society, he cited Tertullian. When he gave a final and sole example of real missionary activity among natives, he deferred to the martyrdom of a good soul. (In Holy Tradition the martyr, or witness, of the faith is the true missionary.) Examples could be multiplied, such as the bishop's native driver's consistent moral behavior, his "orthopraxy" of the Gospel. The Scriptural, Patristic (Church Fathers), and hagiographical (lives of saints) authorities Leskov referenced— applied in context—are familiar and appealing to Orthodox theologians, past and present. (Leskov attained a respectable level of expertise in these areas, so much so that he wrote articles on Patristic commentaries on Scripture and on hagiography.) Whether Leskov would have considered himself

postured for or against the Russian church or the Church univer-
sal during this period is hard to determine with certainty; but
assuredly his critique had a great sensitivity to Holy Tradition,
even if the man himself was not "Orthodox-minded" at the time
of writing.

The only proponent of religious belief Leskov did not take
to task was Leo Tolstoy, although Leskov appears to have had
a more traditional personal faith than Tolstoy. Tolstoy's doctrine, or rather the moralistic positivism of an educated sectarian (complete with an uncritical approach to the gospels as
literature!), was ripe for cross-examination. Nonetheless, late
in life Leskov acceded to Tolstoy's position and claimed it as a
better articulation of his own. In summarizing Leskov's religious questionings, perhaps it is appropriate to remember an
observation of the philosopher Nicholas Berdyaev: Late nineteenth-century Russian literature exhibited a strong religious
and moral character, along with its political and social natures;
and this was an indicator of Russian spiritual life, regardless of
the express personal beliefs of the epoch's authors.

Leskov's sense of irony and command of genres were such
that he would be comfortable expressing a birthday congratula-
tion in the form of a newspaper obituary, leaving the general
readership of the paper to wonder whether the birthday greeting
was "dark humor" or a murder wish. If ironies and table-turn-
ings punctuated his writing, they might have originated in the
conundrums that accentuated his changing personal views. It is
extremely rare, if not unprecedented, that a social critic of
Leskov's caliber could alternately court the political Left, the
ultra-Right, and the Left again; could write pieces disparaging
to Jews, then write paid, pro-Jewish tracts, then write disparaging ones again, and finally be sympathetic; could manage to
offend both the proponents and opponents of a religious movement with the same article (Pashkovists/Radstockists); could
make saints of anti-establishment revolutionaries and ridicule a
man recognized as a saint in his own time (John of Kronstadt);
could be identified as a defender of Orthodoxy and as an anti-
church Tolstoyan; and so on. Surely, all of this did not proceed
simply from an evolved psychological predisposition or a
mercenary's compromise of integrity, though perhaps some of

it did. I suspect that an artistic genius unsure of his personal worth severely tested society time and time again over the years—and most often found it wanting. What was and is valuable in his critical assessments probably provoked his contemporaries because of its accuracy. Besides, no one accused Leskov of being a likeable person. His relationships were seldom lukewarm, and friendships were always fleeting.

Many of the attitudes Leskov expressed through his characters were very unpopular at the time, but now may be viewed, to a certain degree, as prophetic. His affirmation of missionizing natives without supplanting their indigenous languages and cultures, long a professed ideal of Orthodox Christianity, has met with acceptance in recent decades in Roman Catholic and Protestant churches. The work of the Russian Church with the Alaskan natives, begun before Leskov's birth and concluded during his lifetime, stands as a living monument to this ideal today.[3] In particular his stand on traditional iconography as superior to western art for purposes of worship and on the value of Christian education preceding baptism have both been vindicated, albeit recently, within the seminaries of the Orthodox Church. Nevertheless, Leskov is a man of his time; and he expresses typical nineteenth-century, Russian prejudices—usually with cleverness and irony. He is content to disparage groups such as Roman Catholics and borderland native tribes, and to ventilate Russian chauvanistic views towards things non-Russian. These expressions are not characteristic of present-day Russian society or the Russian Orthodox Church, for the most part.

The author is an experienced, master crafter of stories who encourages the reader to embrace the characters in this short

3 During the thirty years after Russia's sale of Alaska to the United States in 1867, the Russian Church spent more money on the education of Alaskan natives than did the U.S. Government. The U.S. government dealt with the natives by suppressing their languages and cultures, separating children from their families, and reeducating them, policies directly opposed to those of the Russian Church. Not only the U.S. government deserves stricture. It should be pointed out that prior to this period the Russian missionaries in Alaska expended considerable energy in protecting the native population from Russian adventurers who had exploited these peoples in other ways.

novel. The narrative is powerful; and given the fact that the book's narrator is based on a historical personage, the appeal is heightened. The combination of an interesting story and superb storywriting makes for a riveting and fascinating reading experience. Most people come away from *On the Edge* with a vivid, lasting memory of particular characters and scenes. Of special note, the snowstorm description in the later chapters is widely recognized as one of the greatest in Russian literature.

The Historical Identity of the Bishop

The question of the identity of the story's narrator is an interesting one, since there were a number of eighteenth- and nineteenth-century missionary bishops whose experiences were similar to those Leskov described. Fortunately, Leskov himself belatedly cleared up the mystery. Archbishop Nil or Nilus (Isakovich) of Irkutsk (1799-1874), and subsequently of Yaroslavl', was one of the more likely candidates. He was author of the analysis, *Buddhism: An Examination of Its Relationship to Its Followers Dwelling in Siberia* (1858, in Russian) and *Travel Notes* (1874), two items which correspond with elements in *On the Edge*; but during the bishop's lifetime Leskov never divulged his secret. Whether out of respect for the man's modesty or privacy, out of regard for the mystique of the historical novel, out of Leskov's deference to his personal ideological agenda, or for some other reason, the question was left unanswered for several years. After Nil's death Leskov indicated the man's connection with the story in the preface to the 1877 essay "Episcopal Justice":

> I no longer see the need to hide the fact that the hierarch from whose memoirs this story was made up was none other than the recently departed Archbishop of Yaroslavl', His Eminence Nil, who himself told the incidents which formerly happened to him, presently under consideration, to one living and thriving in Petersburg, the honorable and trustworthy person, V. A. Kokorev. V.A.Kokorev reported this to me.

Leskov's relationship with the financier-banker V. A. Kokorev (1817-1889) is recorded in the biography, *The Life of Nikolai Leskov*, written by his son, Andrei Leskov. Thus, we may certainly identify the inspiration for the main character of the following pages with Archbishop Nil (Isakovich). [For a description of nineteenth-century Russian missionary work in English, similar in many respects to the above, see Paul Garrett, *St. Innocent: Apostle to America*. Crestwood, NY: SVS Press, 1979.]

✷ The Social and Religious Context

Most western readers assume that the tsarist government in Russia always supported Orthodox Christianity to the exclusion of other faiths during the time of the Empire. The historical record does not entirely confirm this supposition; and the reader should accept as factual the incidents related herein in regard to government interference in support of Buddhism. The winds of government, and we may include here the opinions of the intelligensia as well, blew in many directions in tsarist Russia.

During the eighteenth and nineteenth centuries the spread of Christianity among the peoples of eastern Siberia met with obstacles not only from the side of the old pagan religion under the auspices of shamanism, but also from lamas who competed there with the Russian Orthodox missionaries. The lamas cultivated Buddhism among these peoples in its Tibetan-Mongolian form, so-called lamaism. They easily adapted to prevailing social conditions, included in their pantheon the local gods, and enlarged their cult with the local rites. By the first half of the eighteenth century they obtained from the tsarist government recognition of independent Siberian lamaism, which was advancing as the chief agent of tsarism in Buryat-Mongolia. This accounted for the sympathy shown lamaism by the central, as well as the provincial, governments. In *Buddhism* Nil put forward the entire confrontation with Siberian lamaism:

> Almost no one decided to accept baptism from paganism, afraid of going against the lamas. Besides this, before they were baptized they didn't have any peace. They [the lamas] chased them, they burdened them with all measures... The children grew up idol-worshippers, having Christian parents. Fathers and mothers, formerly Christians, had their faith and betrayed it for paganism in order not to fall into the clutches of the lamas. (p. 254)

Correspondingly, Nil made reference in *Travel Notes* to the situation wherein the Christianization of the indigenous population of Siberia was aided by the Russian imperial military command. He quoted from an ukaz or edict of the Holy Synod to Bishop Benjamin of Irkutsk, dated August 27, 1805:

> His royal, imperial majesty is pleased to make this announcement to the Diocese of Irkutsk and to the Protopresbyter and preacher Gregory Sleptsov of the Nativity of the Mother of God Church in Irkutsk regarding the protection of the military chapel. It was given to you by the royal command for the dissemination of the Faith among the foreign peoples, and in particular, the Chukots. Jurisdiction of the chapel is not to be military—since military arms could disturb the tranquility of the savage peoples and the uneducated—but it is to be civilian.

Sleptsov explained that he was thankful for such help for ten years, 1805-1815, "not less than 1,000 heterodox were converted to Christianity" (pp. 349, 353). Thus, either of these political contexts, government support of Christian missions or government support of Buddhist missions, could occur; and occasionally they existed side-by-side.

Tragically, the lamas often employed violence against the populations, preventing their conversion to Christianity; and unprincipled Christians baptized to command the obedience of their new "godchildren." A "dual-faith" or "two beliefs" sprang up—a mixture of the various religions which were foisted on the natives all at the same time. The term "dual-faith" is a familiar one to the Russian reader, since it was used to describe the popular mixture of Christianity and paganism in ancient Rus' after the conversion of Vladimir. During Nil's tenure as bishop Buddhism, Christianity, and shamanism were mixed together to varying degrees. Such was the religious context we find in the historical period of the present novel.

In order to understand the native peoples which appear throughout the novel, the following brief summaries are offered. Yakut is the Turkic language of the northernmost Turkic people, which people, language, and religion are all known as Yakut. Living in northeastern Siberia in the Lena River basin, they herd horses and cattle, hunt, fish, produce crafts, and trade. Subjugated by Russia in the first half of the seventeenth century, many adopted Christianity by the end of the next century. Nominally Russian Orthodox, some preserved their own shamanism modifying it with Christianity, for example attributing traits of God,

Mary, and angels to shaman spirits—as above, a "dual-faith." In 1979 the Yakut numbered approximately 328,000.

Tungus (or Tunguz) refers to the Tungusic languages of the Tungus peoples, including the Evenki and Eveny among others. Again, the term designates the people, their language, and their religion. This Mongoloid hunting tribe is possibly related to the Manchu, and through small groups dominated the area bordered by the Arctic Ocean on the north, Lake Baikal on the south, the Sea of Okhotsk on the east, and the Yenisei River on the west. Tribal mythology, including myths of creation, heroic deeds, the bear ceremony, etc., is reproduced in their religious ceremony. (See Notes.) Today many of these nomadic groups still exist, numbering about 56,000 individuals in 1979.

The Zyryans (or Zyrians) are known also as Komi, and constitute one of two parts of the Permyak branch of the Finno-Ugric populations of central Russia. In the ninth century the Permians divided into Komi and Udmurts. The Komi still live between the upper Western Dvina River, Kama, and Pechora, a large region west of the northern Urals toward Arkhangel'sk. In 1979 the Komi numbered over 325,000.

Historically, the Komi came into contact with Christianity as early as the twelfth century since they were trading partners with Novgorod. Their conversion is associated with Saint Stephen of Perm (c. 1345-1396), who was a Russian born among the Zyryans. In 1370 after spending thirteen years as a monk at Rostov, Stephen traveled to this people situated east of the Volga. He believed, in concert with Orthodox Tradition, that the people should worship in their own language, so he created an alphabet for them from the line design in their embroidery and carving. Following this, he translated the Bible and the liturgy of the Church from Greek into Zyryan. He also is known to have founded schools and seminaries to train native clergy. For information on the non-Christian religion of the Zyryans see the articles "Finnic Religions" and "Finno-Ugric Religions" in *The Encyclopedia of Religion* edited by Mircea Eliade.

The Genre

The genre, or type of literature, represented by *On the Edge* is the Leskovian *skaz*, meaning a tale within a tale. The general term *skaz* is a bit more complicated than this brief description, of course, but it may be approximated here.[4] This type of literature has a formal frame, begun by a first narrator, and then an internal unit or kernel which is told by a storyteller—a story ostensibly told orally by a second narrator. The last part of the frame, or the end of the novel, is completed by the first narrator, however short a conclusion. One way in which this novel departs from the *skaz* more broadly defined is that the story is not told by an unlettered person having the appeal of local color, but on the contrary, by an educated, cultivated churchman of high rank. Another more traditional *skaz* by Leskov is *The Night Owls* (*Polunoshchniki*). As examples of literature with similar genre characteristics, the story within a story, one might call to mind the Book of Job[5] or *The Canterbury Tales*. Each of these contains a first narrator's frame within which the principal story, or stories, is secondarily told.

Certain characteristics of the Leskovian *skaz* provide us with insights into the author's technique. First, the frame is always shorter and more formal, using polished language and a more sophisticated vocabulary, than the "oral" story which it frames. The single episode surrounded by a frame has very much the tone and color of a story told orally. It has been made to "sound like" a storyteller's tale by the choice of vocabulary, colloquialisms, narrative technique, etc. Though the internal kernel of the *skaz* approximates a tale told orally, it is in fact literary, or a literary device, and not oral speech—which may be ascertained by reading the text aloud. (If only casual speech were as lively and varied as that of Leskov's characters!)

4 The technical definition of the Leskovian *skaz* is, "stylistically individualized inner narrative placed in the mouth of a fictional character and designed to produce the illusion of oral speech." Hugh McLean, "On the Style of a Leskovian *Skaz*," *Harvard Slavic Studies*, II (Cambridge, MA, 1954), p. 299.

5 That is to say, the original ending of Job is, according to most scholars, the final speech of God. Thus, the structure of Job is a) the first frame section, the discussion in the heavenly council, b) the internal oral units, the dialogues of Job and his friends, and c) the second frame section, the theophanic answer of God. Under this reconstruction the ending, wherein Job receives everything back, and the discourse of Elihu, which clearly anticipates God's theophanic answer, are considered as secondary accretions to the original.

Second, Leskov used the *skaz* genre "politically" to distance himself, somewhat, from controversial ideas he wanted to express. The Russian imperial and ecclesiastical censors frequently were unable to discover Leskov's own "subversive" opinions, since they were voiced by characters seemingly twice-removed from the author. In the present work, for example, the consistent and poignant critique of practices of the nineteenth-century Russian church are greatly softened in the perception of the reader when spoken by a monk who was willing to die for his faith or by an old archbishop whose Orthodoxy and allegiance were not in question. If that critique stood alone, without the sympathetic reading ensured by the set-up of the genre, it might have proved overbearing, an unacceptable affront, and as a result would not have been printed. Curiously, Leskov was aware of the fact that his readers more often took away entertaining memories and an appreciation of character portrayals from his writings—in spite of camouflaged deeper meanings and hidden agendas—than they did his latest social commentary.

The Translation

Finally, a few words are in order regarding this translation. My aim was to be as faithful as possible to the original Russian, using modern idiomatic American English, while avoiding a paraphrastic translation style. Particular dialects, without a doubt, could not be reproduced; but proper and improper grammar, earthiness and hominess, and a propensity for slang could. One criterion used in translating was whether the words were believable speech in a particular character's mouth, respecting the strength of Leskov's personifications and their consistent word coloration. As an added check I attempted to maintain the approximate number of words and variation in vocabulary which occur in the Russian, so that the length of narrative and dialogue corresponds closely to the original.

In the many places Leskov has placed incorrect or awkward speech in the mouths of his characters, I have put forward incorrect or awkward English equivalents. Also, where Leskov has lured the reader by using a new pronoun without any apparent antecedent, creating anticipation or tension, I have done the same. The technique involved is a simple and effective one, but sometimes leaves the reader with the impression he has missed something. He has, but by the author's design; and usually the contrived question is answered momentarily.

In an early draft of this translation I attempted to preserve all of Leskov's method and style of punctuation—which seems to contribute favorably to the illusion of "orality" or oral speech. Everyone who read the draft agreed that the punctuation proved too cumbersome for the modern reader, especially since the conventions of style of nineteenth-century Russia are so different from our own. Nevertheless, wherever practical I did try to maintain the author's propensity for sentences punctuated by dashes and suspension points (dots or ellipsis points). In the frequent cases where suspension points are found in the Russian text it is not always clear what Leskov had in mind: a pause in speech, an interruption, a break in thought, an unrecorded piece of obvious dialogue, or simply a trailing off of the conversation. Although Leskov's usage of suspension points goes beyond the definitions of the manuals of style for proper English—or Russian, for that matter—it seemed prudent to maintain his own system with its flexibility and ambiguities, since he clearly intended it as a feature of his art.

The transliteration of Russian words follows the Library of Congress system unless superseded by convention. The Notes after the last chapter are designed to be a handy reference to persons, places, etc., which otherwise might be unfamiliar to the reader. Footnotes provide vital information in a word or short phrase.

On the Edge of the World has been read in the Russian emigré community, the now-defunct Soviet Union, and Germany, and is seen cited from time to time in secular and theological literature. An earlier English language translation—available in Chamot's *The Sentry* from 1922—is literally accurate, for the most part, but difficult to obtain and, by now, dated. Some years ago Mr. Andrew Rayburn shared his personal translation of the novel with me and I was immediately captivated. I am indebted to both Chamot and Rayburn for the work they have done and for their appreciation of Leskov and his inimitable characters. Important to the present work are the Russian text and the invaluable notes provided by L. B.

Domanovsky in the Soviet edition of Leskov's collected works
[V.G. Bazanov, et al., eds., *N.S. Leskov: Sobranie Sochinenii*,
Tom 5 (Moskva: Gosudarstvennoe Izdatel'stvo Xudozhestvennoi
Literatury, 1957)] which are the basis of a number of entries in
the Notes and of Archbishop Nil's writings, to which I did not
have direct access.

I would like to thank the many people without whose help
this translation would not have been possible. First are Professors Olga Raevsky-Hughes and Hugh McLean of the University
of California, Berkeley, Department of Slavic Languages and
Literatures, without whose encouragement, kind direction, cor-
rections, and suggestions I would have foundered. Professor
McLean's book on Leskov, *Nikolai Leskov: The Man and His
Art* (Cambridge, Massachusetts: Harvard University Press,
1977, 780 pp.), will long remain the standard in Leskov studies.
At this point mention is in order of the work of the I. V.
Koulaieff Educational Foundation, not only at U.C. Berkeley,
but throughout communities in the San Francisco Bay area.
Next, my mother-in-law, Valentina Gogol, provided me with
practical day-to-day help, clues to word meanings in addition to
dialect—Leskov liked to use words that do not appear in dic-
tionaries—and invaluable readings by a native speaker and
literature lover. My wife, Margaret, listened to rough translations and typed manuscripts. Three old friends, all experts in
their own right, proofread the final drafts. Michael D. Peterson,
Branch Librarian at the San Anselmo collection of the Graduate
Theological Union, provided research help; and Dr. Kathryn A.
Klar of the Celtic Studies Program, U.C. Berkeley, and Archpriest Vadim Pogrebniak, rector of Saint Spiridon Cathedral,
Seattle, both made worthwhile recommendations. All mistakes
and shortcomings are my own.

31 December 1991
Feast of Saint Melanie
Pacific Lutheran Theological Seminary
Berkeley, California

Chapter One

Early one evening during the Christmas holidays we were taking tea in the large blue sitting room of the archbishop's residence. There were seven of us, the eighth being the host, an archbishop well-advanced in years, now sick and infirm. The guests were all intellectuals and an interesting conversation began among them on our faith and faithlessness, on preaching in our churches, and on the enlightening work of our missionaries in the East. Numbered among the company was a certain Captain B. of the Navy, a very good fellow, but also a great antagonist of the Russian clergy. He reiterated that our missionaries were absolutely incapable of their task; and he was glad that the government had now decided to allow foreign evangelical pastors to propagate the Word of God. B. asserted his firm conviction that these preachers would not only enjoy great success among us, especially among the Jews, but would show—as surely as two and two make four—the incapacity of the Russian clergy for missionary preaching.

Our respected host remained profoundly silent during the course of this conversation. He sat in his large, Voltairian armchair, his legs covered by a plaid quilt, and—to all appearances—was thinking about something else; but when B. finished, the old archbishop sighed and continued the talk: "It seems to me, gentlemen, that you might have wrongly become contentious with our good Captain. I think he's right. Foreign missionaries positively must have great success among us."

"I am very happy, Your Eminence, that you share my opinion," Captain B. responded, and proceeded to add a few of the most seemly and delicate compliments to the archbishop's reputation for intellectual cultivation and nobility of character.

"To be sure, Your Eminence, you know better than I all the shortcomings of the Russian Church, where among the clergy there are, of course, people who are very intelligent and very good—I don't begin to dispute that—but, they hardly understand Christ. Their situation and so on...compels them to interpret everything...too narrowly."

The Archbishop looked at him, smiled and answered, "Yes, good Captain, my modesty doesn't suffer when I say that I know the sorrows of the Church perhaps not less than you; but the truth might suffer if I were to agree with you that our Lord Christ is understood less in Russia than in Tübingen, London, or Geneva."

"About this it's still possible to argue, Your Eminence."

The Archbishop again smiled and said, "You, I see, are sporting for an argument. What shall we do with you! We decline to argue, but let's talk about it—here we are."

And with this he took from the table a large album, richly decorated with carved ivory, and he opened it saying, "Here is our Lord! I call you to look! Here I gathered many portrayals of His face. Here He sits by the well with the Samaritan woman—a wonderful work. The artist, one must think, understood...the face, the moment."

"Yes. To me too it seems, Your Eminence, that this was done with understanding," B. answered.

"However, isn't there superfluous softness in the divine face? Doesn't it seem to you that He is too complacent concerning how many husbands this woman had, and that her current husband is not her husband?"

Everyone got quiet. The Archbishop, noticing this, continued, "It seems to me that here a little stricter attention would not be amiss."

"You're right, it's possible, Your Eminence."

"Another widely known picture—I frequently have occasion to see it, chiefly at the ladies' place. Let us examine further. Again, a great master. Christ here is kissed by Judas. What does the face of the Lord seem like to you here? Such reserve and kindness! Isn't it so? A wonderful portrayal!"

"A wonderful face!"

every man inscribes on thensilvs on God

"However, here isn't there a bit too much effort to achieve self-control? Look. The left cheek seems to me to tremble and the mouth, possibly, shows disgust."

"Of course it's there, Your Eminence."

"Oh, yes. Yes, well, Judas deserved it to be sure, both a servant and a flatterer. He was very capable of evoking that reaction from anyone...only, however, not from Christ, Who did not disdain anything, but felt pity for all. Well, we shall let it pass. This one, it seems, does not quite satisfy us, although I know a very high official who told me that he could not conceive of a more felicitous portrayal of Christ. Here is Christ once more, and from the brush of a master as well, Titian. Before the Lord stands the wily Pharisee, denarius in hand. Look. What a cunning old man, but Christ...Christ...Oh, I fear! Look. Isn't there contempt on His face?"

"It's possible, Your Eminence."

"That it's possible, I won't argue. The old man is a vile creature; but when I pray, I don't have such an idea of the Lord and find this one discomforting—don't you agree?"

We expressed agreement, finding it discomforting to imagine Christ with such an expression, particularly when offering Him prayers.

"I'm absolutely in agreement with you in this, and I even recollect arguing about it with one diplomat who liked only *this* Christ; but, however, what?...a diplomatic moment. But let's proceed further. From here on there are portrayals of Christ alone, without any accompanying figures. Here is a photograph for you of a wonderful bust by the sculptor Cauer: Good, good!—no question; say what you like, but to me this academic bust resembles Christ far less than it does Plato. Here He is again...what a sufferer...what a horrible countenance Metsu has given Him!...I don't understand, why did he beat, flog, and wound Him so?...It's truly terrible! Eyelids swollen, blood and bruises...all the breath, it seems, has been beaten out of Him and it's even terrible to look at a body which suffers so...We turn the page quickly. At this point He inspires only compassion and nothing more. —Here is Lafond, perhaps not a great artist, but he is liked by many nowadays. He, as you see, understood Christ differently from all the foregoing, and differently repre-

sented Him to us: a figure slender and winning, a good face,
dove-like beneath a pure brow, and how lightly his hair is blown
now, here curls, here these ringlets twirled, lying on His brow.
Beautiful, true! And in His hand a heart glows, entwined with
thorns. This is the 'Sacré coeur' which the Jesuit fathers preach.
Someone told me that they inspired Mr. Lafond to portray
Christ in this way; however, it is liked also by people who think
they have nothing in common with the Jesuits. I remember once
during a severe freeze I had occasion to visit one Russian prince
in Petersburg who showed me the wonders of his mansion, and
there it was, not quite in its proper place—in a winter garden, I
saw this Christ for the first time. The picture stood on a table in
a small frame, in front of which the princess was sitting lost in
dreams. It was a wonderful setting: palms, arums, bananas,
birds chirping and fluttering about and she daydreamed. About
what? She told me, 'In search of Christ.' I then took a good look
at this picture. Really, you see, He comes forth from the background by visual effect, or it's better to say, He emerges out of
this darkness. Behind Him is nothing—none of those prophets
who pester everyone, running around in their rags and even
clinging to the king's chariot wheels, none of this, but only
darkness...the darkness of fantasy. This lady—the Lord
strengthen her—first explained to me the secret of how to find
Christ, after which I would not argue with the good Captain that
foreign preachers among us will show Him not just to Jews, but
to all, to all who desire that He would come under palm and
banana tree to listen to canaries. Only would He come there?
Wouldn't someone else come to them in His guise? I must
confess to you, I would readily prefer this Jewish-looking head
by Guercino to the dandified, 'canary' Christ, though
Guercino's only speaks to me of a good and enthusiastic rabbi
whom, according to the formulation of Mr. Renan, one could
love and listen to with pleasure...And here you are, how many
understandings and presentations of Him, Who alone is needed
by all of us! Now let's close this pictorial album, and turn your
eyes to the icon corner which is directly behind you. Again the
image of Christ which this time is not called a face—but an
image. Here is the typical Russian representation of the Lord.
The look of His face is straightforward and simple, the crown

of the head is elevated which, as is even well-known according
to the system of Lavater, signifies the capacity for elevated
respect for God; the face has expression but not passion. How
did our old masters attain to such a fascinating representation?
—This remains their secret which died along with them and
their rejected art. Simplicity—to desire more simplicity in art is
impossible. The lines are barely indicated but they make a full
impression. He is a bit peasant-like, to be sure, but all the same
He inspires veneration. People may differ, but in my opinion
our simple-hearted master *understood* better than anyone—Him
Whom he had to paint. He is a bit peasant-like, I repeat, and He
will not be invited to listen to canaries in a winter garden, but
never mind—in whatever form He revealed Himself, there He
will walk in that form; but us He visited in the form of a servant
and so He walks, with no place to lay His head, from Petersburg
to Kamchatka. Evidently it pleases Him to accept abuse with
those of us who drink His blood and also shed it. And thus, in
my opinion, to the extent that our people's art has more simply
and successfully understood the outward features of the portrayal of Christ, perhaps our people's spirit has better perceived
the truth of the inward features of His character. If you like I
shall tell you of a related experience which perhaps is not
entirely devoid of interest."

"Oh, please do, Your Eminence. We all entreat you to do
so!"

"Ah, you entreat me?—Very well. Then I entreat you to
listen and not interrupt, for my story begins afar off."

We cleared our throats, settled in our places in order not to
stir, and the Archbishop began.

authenticity, stripped of ideology
social frills, drama and Romance
truth lies in simplicity

Chapter Two

"We must be transported back, gentlemen, to a time when—
you might say—I was still a fairly young man and was
consecrated bishop and assigned to a very remote Siberian
diocese. I had an ardent disposition by nature and loved to have
many things to do, so that's why I was not only not saddened,
but was even thrilled by this far-off assignment. Thank God, I
thought, that for the start my lot was not only to tonsure ordinands or investigate drunken readers, but to begin a genuine
life's work, with which it was possible to occupy oneself with
devotion. I mean by this the same marginally successful missionary efforts which the Captain deigned to point out at the
beginning of the present discussion. I traveled to my new assignment fired with zeal and with the most extensive plans; and
suddenly all my ardor cooled. What is still more important, I
came within an inch of spoiling the whole affair, had a miraculous event not given me a salvific lesson."

"Miraculous!" exclaimed one of the listeners, forgetting the
agreement not to interrupt the story; but our indulgent host
didn't become angry at this and answered:

"Yes, gentlemen, the word slipped out, and I do not have to
take it back. In what happened to me and that which I am about
to relate—it's not without the miraculous, and these miracles
seemed to me to begin almost on the very first day of my arrival
in my semi-savage diocese. The first thing which a Russian
bishop does when he begins his occupational work, wherever he
may find himself, is of course a survey of the appearance of the
churches and the religious services, to which I applied myself.
I ordered spare Gospels and crosses to be removed from altars
everywhere, thanks to which our altars are often turned into
something like store windows of ecclesiastical accoutrements.
I ordered a number of eagle rugs, as many as necessary to be

29

installed in all their proper places, so that the subdeacons would
not run to and fro around me, tossing them under my feet. With
effort and under threat of severe punishment I restrained the
deacons from grabbing me by the elbows during the liturgical
services and also from perching next to me at the high place, but
most of all from cuffing and squeezing the backs or the necks
of the poor ordinands, who for about two weeks after receiving
the grace of the Holy Spirit had sore backs and necks. And none
of you would believe what difficulties and vexations this
brought, especially to an impatient man, such as I was then and
so remain partly hitherto, to my shame. Finishing this, I had to
undertake the second episcopal task of the first importance: to
make sure whether those who are to be tonsured reader know
how to read, if not smoothly then at least correctly. These
examinations kept me busy for a long while and greatly annoyed me, though from time to time they made me laugh. An
illiterate reader or sacristan, as they say an "unlettered" one,
may now still be found in a village or in the chief town of a
small district in the interior of Russia, as was demonstrated
when a few years ago they had for the first time to sign pay
vouchers for their salaries. But then—in those olden days, and
what's more in Siberia—this was a most common occurrence. I
ordered them to study. They, of course, complained of me and
called me 'cruel,' a despot; the parishes complained that there
were no readers, that the bishop was 'ruining the churches.'
What was I to do! I began to supply in place of such readers
those who at least knew the service books by heart, and—oh,
God!—what sort of people I saw! Squint-eyed, lame, nasal-
toned, fools, and even... some possessed. One, in place of the
prayer, 'Come let us worship God, our King,' would close his
eyes and call like a quail, 'Comlswirshpgod, comlswirshpgod';
and he got so carried away with it that it was impossible to
restrain him. Another—this one really was possessed—was so
seduced by his own fast reading that with some well-known
words, associated ideas occurred to him, which he was in no
way able to control. For example, for him such a phrase would
be 'in heaven.' He would begin to read the prayer, 'Thou who
at all times and at every hour in heaven'... and all of a sudden
something would snap in his head, and he would continue,

'hallowed be Thy Name, Thy Kingdom come.' What torment I went through with him, and all in vain! I ordered him to read by the book. He read, 'Thou who at all times and at every hour in heaven,' but suddenly shut the book and continued, 'hallowed be Thy Name,' and muttered to the end, and then exclaimed, 'but deliver us from Evil.' Only here was he able to come to a full stop. It turned out that he didn't know how to read. After the matter of the literacy of the readers we moved in turn to the good conduct of the seminarians, and again the wonders never ceased. The ordinary seminary was so undisciplined—the pupils got drunk and so disorderly during divine services—that, for example, one undergraduate student finished the evening prayers in the presence of the inspector by reading, 'The Father is my hope, the Son is my refuge, the Holy Spirit is my protection. O Holy Trinity—my compliments to You.' Yet another situation occurred in the graduate class. One theological student gave thanks after dinner with the prayer, 'Thou hast satisfied us with Thy earthly blessings, deprive us not of Thy Heavenly Kingdom'; but one of the crowd yelled at him, 'Swine! You stuffed yourself and still ask to get into the Heavenly Kingdom.'"

It was necessary to try to find an inspector as soon as possible, one who would fit in with my approach—also despotic. With time short and choices limited one such turned up. There was plenty of despotism in him, but it was no use asking for anything else.

He says, "I, Your Grace, shall do all of this in military fashion, in order to immediately...."

"Fine," I answer, "do it in military fashion...."

So he did. He begins by ordering that the prayers before meals not be read but sung by a choir, in order to eliminate all pranks and to sing by his command. He rises in complete silence, and everyone is quiet until he begins to conduct. He gives the order, "Prayer!" and they begin to sing. But he carried the "militarization" even further. He orders, "Pray-yer!" The seminarians only begin singing, "The eyes of all, O Lord, are upon Th—," when he yells, "Sto-op," in the middle of a word and calls one of them forward.

"Frolov, come here!"

The man approaches.

"Are you Bagreyev?"

"No, I'm Frolov."

"Aha. Are you Frolov?! Then why did I think that you are Bagreyev?"

Laughter ensued—and again complaints came to me. No, I saw that this inspector with his military techniques would not do; and I somehow found a civilian who, though not so much a despot, acted more sensibly. Before the students he feigned being a good old soul, but to me he told tales about everything they did, and everywhere else told horrifying stories of my brutality. I knew all that, and seeing that this technique proved itself workable, did not oppose his system.

hypocrisy

I had no sooner reduced the seminarians to some degree of obedience by "despotism," when wonders began to occur among those of mature age. They informed me that a cartload of hay had *entered into* the rector[1] of the cathedral and could not exit. I sent to find out what happened; and they said it really had happened. The rector was obese. Following the liturgy he had performed a baptism in the home of a merchant and afterward had generously treated himself to some homemade liqueur; and this, like many others made from local wild berries, produced the greatest and most stupefying intoxication. Added to this he went home, slept about four hours, got up and drank a jug of kvas,[2] and lay hanging part-way out a window in order to talk with someone standing down below; and suddenly...a cartload of hay drove into him. You know, all of this was so stupid that it began to be disgusting, but before it was through it became even a bit more disgusting. The next day my aid brought me my boots and reported, "Thank God, by now the cartload of hay has backed out of Father Rector."

"I'm very glad," I said, "such joy; but give me the story in detail."

It turns out that the rector, having a two-story house, had lain in the window right over the gate, where just at that moment a cartload of hay was coming in. It seemed to him—be-

1 Literally, archpriest or protopresbyter.
2 A weak, homemade beer or cider-like drink made by pouring warm water over a mixture of cereals, bread, or fruit and allowing it to ferment.

cause of the liqueur and the stupor of sleep—that it had driven into him. Strange but true: *Credo, quia absurdum.*[3]

How did they save this wonder-working man?

By another wonder: He would not agree to stand up because the cart was inside him. The doctor could not find a remedy for his malady. So they summoned a shamaness to help. She spun herself around, knocked, and ordered the cartload of hay outside to be loaded and backed out. The sick man accepted the premise that the load had backed out of him and recovered.

Well, after this you could do for him what you will, but he had already done himself in. He both made a laughingstock of himself before the people and summoned the shamaness to treat him with idolatrous sorcery; and such things are not hidden under a bushel but are shouted from the housetops.[4] "The priests—what good are they when they themselves call our shamans to drive off shaitan."[5] Such nonsense went on and on. For a considerable time I trimmed these smokey icon-lamps[6] as much as I could, and because of it the parochial part of my work ate away insufferably at me; but long after this came the desired and wished-for moment, when I was able to devote myself entirely to the work of the enlightenment of the wild sheep of my flock, who were pasturing without a pastor.

I collected all the pertinent paperwork on the subject and sat over it in earnest, so that I did not get up from my desk.

---

3 "I believe because it is absurd." —Tertullian
4 The saying Leskov used means literally, "Such things do not lie there in a little sack but rather run along the road."
5 An evil spirit, a rebellious jinn which leads people astray.
6 Church candles lit before icons.

Chapter Three

Having familiarized myself with the missionaries' reports, I was left more dissatisfied with all their activities than with the activities of my parish clergy. Conversions to Christianity were extraordinarily few, and it was also clear that a good portion of these conversions existed only on paper. But the fact was that some of the baptized returned again to their former faith—lamaism or shamanism—while others made the strangest and most absurd mixture of all these faiths. They prayed to Christ and His apostles, and Buddha and his bodhisattvas, and to *tengerins*,[1] and *angons*.[2] Not only nomads adhered to the "dual-faith," but it was almost everywhere in my flock, which did not represent a separate branch of a certain people but some such bits and pieces of many tribes. God knows when and whence the variety of tribes came here, with limited speech and still poorer understanding and imagination. Seeing that everything pertinent to missionary work was in such chaos here, I formed the most unfavorable opinion of my fellow workers and treated them with harsh impatience. On the whole I became very irritable and the nickname "despot" given me began to fit. The poor little monastery I chose for my residence and where I wanted to found a school for natives suffered especially from my angry impatience. Asking around among the monks, I found out that almost everyone in the town spoke Yakut, but of my monks only one very aged hieromonk,[3] Father Kiriak, spoke any foreign language, though he too was not suited for the work of preaching; and if he was suited, even under pain of death he didn't want to go preach to the savages.

1 Shamanistic spirits which personify nature, the elements, etc.
2 Shamanistic spirits which personify spirits of dead ancestors.
3 A monk ordained a priest.

"What does this mean," I asked, "and how dare he be so disobedient? He must be told I don't like it and won't tolerate it."

The ecclesiarch[4] answered that my message would be conveyed, but he added that it's useless to expect obedience from Kiriak since it's not the first time this has happened. Two of my predecessors, quickly succeeding one another, tried disciplining him severely, but he took his stand and answered both the same:

"I would gladly lay down my life for my Christ, but I shall not go baptize there (that is, in the wilderness)." He even said that it would be better to be defrocked than to be sent out there. And he was deprived of his priestly office many years for this disobedience, though he didn't find it hard in the least, but the opposite. He did the most menial tasks with joy: at one time watchman, at another bellringer. And he is loved by all, both the brothers and the lay people, and even the heathens.

"How? I am surprised. Is it possible, even the heathens?"

"Yes, Your Grace, some of the heathens come to him even now."

"For what purpose?"

"They respect him from the old days, when he formerly went about preaching."

"And what kind of man was he then, in those former times?"

"Then he was the most successful missionary and converted a great number of people."

"What was it that happened to him? What caused him to abandon this work?"

"It's impossible to understand, Your Grace. All of a sudden something happened to him. He returned from the steppes, placed the Chrism and Holy Communion kits on the altar and said, 'I am putting these here and shall not take them up again until the hour comes.'"

"What sort of hour does he need? What does he mean by it?"

"I don't know, Your Grace."

4 An official more usually found in monasteries than in parishes who is approximately equivalent to a sacristan.

"And is it possible that none of you could extract it from him? O, evil generation, how long shall I be with you and endure you? How is it that these pertinent things don't interest you? Remember, if the Lord promised to spew from His mouth those who are neither hot nor cold, how will He reward you who are totally cold?"

But my ecclesiarch justified himself. "In every way possible, Your Grace, did we try to satisfy our curiosity about him, but his answer was always the same: 'No, little children,' he said, 'this matter is no joke—it's terrible...I can't look at it.'"

But what was so terrible about it the ecclesiarch was unable to explain, but only said, "We suppose that Father Kiriak received some sort of revelation while preaching." That made me angry. I confess that I have no sympathy for the assortment of "reputed saints" who perform miracles in this life and boast of having direct revelations, and I have reasons for not liking them. That's why I immediately summoned this refractory Kiriak—not content with my existing reputation for severity and despotism—and then put a grim frown on my face. I was ready to scorch him with my anger when he came into sight. But when this monk appeared before my eyes—so small, so quiet— it wasn't even possible to shoot a glare at him; dressed in a faded calico cassock, his klobuk[5] covered in broadcloth, of dark complexion, an alert face, yet he entered cheerfully, without any trepidation, and greeted me first.

"Good day, Your Grace!"

I didn't reply to his greeting, but began sternly, "Are you trying to be original here, friend?"

"How, Your Grace?" he said. "Forgive me, be patient. I'm a little hard of hearing—I didn't get it all."

I repeated myself a bit louder. "Now do you understand?"

"No, I understand nothing," he said.

"And why don't you want to go preach and instead run away from baptizing natives?"

"I went and baptized, Your Grace," he said, "when I didn't have any experience."

5 The monastic head covering with the appearance of a fez with veil, similar to the cowl of the Western Church.

"Yes," I said, "but did you receive experience and stop?"

"I stopped."

"What was your reason?"

He sighed and answered, "The reason is in my heart, Your Grace, and the Seer-of-hearts sees it, that it's too great for me and beyond my feeble strength...I can't!"

And with this he bowed to the ground at my feet.

I raised him up and said, "You shouldn't bow to me, but explain: If and what kind of revelation did you receive or did you talk with God Himself?"

He answered with a gentle reproach, "Don't laugh, Your Grace. I'm not Moses, the Chosen One of God, that it's possible for me to talk with God. It's a sin for you to think so."

I was ashamed of my anger, mollified it, and said to him, "What then? What's the matter?"

"Well, this matter, apparently," he answered, "that I'm not Moses, Your Grace, that I'm timid and know my own limited strengths. I may lead them out of heathen Egypt, but I shall not part the Red Sea and lead them from the steppes and set simple souls murmuring—to the offense of the Holy Spirit."

Noticing figurativeness like this in his colloquial speech, I concluded that he very likely had been an Old Believer,[6] so I asked, "And by what miracle did you yourself enter into the Church?"

He said, "I was united to Her in my infancy and shall abide with Her right to the grave."

Then he told me of his very simple yet very strange beginnings. His father was a priest, early a widower. He had performed some kind of uncanonical wedding and was deprived of his parish, so that his entire life he was unable to find another for himself anywhere; but he attached himself to a certain elderly, important lady, who traveled from place to place her whole life. She, afraid to die without the sacraments, took her priest with her wherever she went. Whenever she goes somewhere—he sits in the front of the carriage with her; whenever she enters a home—he waits for her in the antechamber with the

6 A religious group considered to be archaic and sectarian, and condemned as such ecclesiastically and politically.

servants. Can you imagine a man spending his whole life this way! But meanwhile he, not having his own altar, literally lives off his priest's traveling sacramentary kit, which he keeps with him at all times over his heart, and begs some crumbs from this lady in order to keep his young son in school. That's how they ended up in Siberia. The mistress traveled there to visit her daughter who was married to the provincial governor, and she took the priest with traveling sacramentary kit along in her carriage. But since the trip was long and because the lady was preparing to stay there a while, the priest, who loved his young son, refused to go without him. The lady thought and thought—and seeing that she was unable to prevail over parental love, agreed to take the boy with her. So he traveled from Europe to Asia on the back of the carriage, having as his responsibility on this long trip the protection by his very presence of the attached footman's trunk—to which he himself was lashed, in order that he wouldn't become drowsy and fall off. In Siberia both the lady and his father died, and he was left alone. Due to poverty he never finished his schooling, but ended up a soldier, a prison escort guard. Having a sharp eye, under a direct order, and not properly aiming, he shot a bullet at an escapee; and, without wanting to, and to his own distress, killed him. Ever since then he suffered so terribly and felt so unhappy about everything that he became unfit for service and entered a monastery. Here his excellent conduct was noticed, while his knowledge of the native language and his religiosity naturally inclined him toward missionary work.

I listened to the old man's simple but touching story and felt immense pity for him. In order to change my tone with him I said, "So this is how it came about that they suspected you saw some miracles, isn't that right?"

But he answered, "Why shouldn't it be true, Your Grace?"

"What? ...then you did see miracles?"

"Who hasn't seen miracles, Your Grace?"

"You don't say?"

"Why not? Look anywhere—everything's a miracle: water floats in the clouds; the air holds the earth like a feather. Here we are, you and I, dust and ashes, but we move and think. And that to me is miraculous. We shall die and our dust will be scattered, but our souls will go to Him Who placed them in us. And that to me is miraculous. How does the soul go naked, without anything? Who could give it wings like a dove, to fly to its rest?"

"Well, this we'll leave for others to decide, but you tell me without equivocation: Have you experienced some extraordinary phenomena in your life or something to that effect?"

"Sort of."

"What was it?"

"Since childhood I have been greatly affected by the Grace of God, Your Grace," he said. "Though unworthy, I twice received divine intervention."

"Hm? Do tell."

"The first time, Your Grace, was in early childhood. I was still in the third grade and very much wanted to go outside into the fields. Three of us boys went to ask the principal for recess. Since we didn't receive permission we decided to lie, and I was the instigator of the whole episode. 'C'mon guys,' I said, 'let's fool everybody, we'll run and holler: He let us out, he let us out!' That's what we did; when we hollered everyone ran from class and went out to hike and swim and fish. But toward evening I got really scared. What will happen to me when we get home? —The principal will beat us to death. I got back home and looked—already the switches were soaking in the tub. I quickly beat it to the bathhouse, hid myself under a bench, and, well, began to pray, 'Lord! I know that it's impossible not to be flogged, but make it so they won't flog me!' And I prayed so fervently about this that in the ardor of my faith perspiration broke out and I grew weak; but suddenly there came a breath of wonderful, peaceful, cool air, and my heart was astir like a warm dove, and I began to believe in the impossibility of salvation as a possibility, and I felt peace and such courage that I wasn't afraid of anything, and that's that! And so I lay down to sleep. And when I awoke, I heard my buddies happily yelling, 'Kiriushka! Kiriushka![7] Where are you? C'mon out fast. They won't give you a whipping, the school superintendent came and let us out to play.'"

7 The diminutive or familiar of Kiriak.

"Your miracle," I said, "is a simple one."

"Simple it is, Your Grace, like the Trinity itself in its unity—simple existence," he answered. And he added with indescribable bliss in his eyes, "And you know, Your Grace, how I did feel His presence! How He came to me, my Heavenly Father! How He brought me wonderment and such joy. Judge for yourself. He Who encompasses the whole universe, seeing the grief of a child, creeps up to a boy under a bathhouse bench bringing refreshing coolness to his soul and abiding in his little bosom...."

I must confess to you that more than all the other representations of the Deity I love this one, our *Russian God*, Who makes for Himself an abode in one's 'little bosom.' Whether or not we are obligated to the Greeks because we know of God through them—you can't demonstrate or prove that the Greeks revealed Him to us. We found Him neither in the magnificence of Byzantium nor in the smoke of the censer, but He is simply our own co-sufferer walking everywhere with us, and without incense He fills a soul with a fresh breath under a bathhouse bench, and turns into a dove in one's warm bosom.

"Continue, Father Kiriak," I said, "I'm waiting for the story of the other miracle."

"Right away with the other one, Your Grace. It was as I became more distant from Him through lack of faith. It happened while I was on the way here, riding behind the carriage. They had to take me out of school in European Russia and transfer me here just before the final exam. I wasn't afraid because I was at the head of the class and they would've accepted me into the seminary without an examination; but the principal goes and writes me up a 'satisfactory' transfer recommendation. 'This,' he said, 'is purposely for the reputation of our school, so that when they examine you there they will see what sort of student we consider "satisfactory."' This was a terrible blow to my father and me; but Father wanted me to cram, so that along the road I sat on the footman's trunk and studied. But once I dozed off while we were fording a river and lost all my books. Himself crying bitterly, Father whipped me soundly for it at the wayside inn; but all the same, while we were going to Siberia I forgot about everything and again began

to pray like a child: 'Lord, help me! Make it so they accept me
without an examination.' No, it was not to be as I asked Him.
They looked at my recommendation and ordered me to be examined. I arrived sorrowful. All the other kids were happy and
leapfrogged over one another. I alone was sad, and another
skinny, scrawny boy, who sat without studying and said it was
out of weakness, 'The fever got me.' I sat there gazing into a
book and in my mind began squabbling with the Lord. 'Well,
what now?' I thought. 'You already know what I asked You, but
You didn't do anything!' And with this I got up to go get a drink
of water, when suddenly *bang* on the back of the head, something threw me to the floor in the middle of the room...I thought,
'This is really some punishment! First God didn't give me any
help, then on top of it He hit me.' Then I looked, oh no: It was
only the sick boy who took it into his head to jump over me, but
he wasn't strong enough and he fell and knocked me down.
Then the other kids said to me, 'Look, new kid, your arm isn't
hanging right.' I tried it and the arm was broken. They took me
to the hospital and put me in bed. Father got there and said,
'Don't grieve, Kiriushka, because of this they'll accept you now
without an examination.' Right then I understood how God had
arranged everything, and began to cry...But the examination
was easy, so easy that I could've passed it in my sleep. The
moral: I didn't know, being foolish, what I asked for, but
nevertheless my wish was granted so that I would learn a lesson."

"Oh, Father Kiriak, Father Kiriak," I said, "you are an
extraordinarily consoling human being!...." We thrice exchanged the kiss of peace. I let him go without asking anything
further, and told him to come back the next day to begin teaching me the Tungus and Yakut languages.

Chapter Four

Having abandoned my attitude of severity toward Kiriak, I made up for it by falling upon the other monks of our small monastery—in whom I saw, it's true to say, neither the simplicity of soul of Kiriak nor things useful in service to the faith. They lived at such an advanced post of Christianity, so to speak, in a land of heathenism, but the lazy beggars didn't do anything—not even one of them took the trouble to learn the native language.

I admonished them, admonished them privately at first, and finally thundered at them from the pulpit[1] with the words of Tsar Ivan which were addressed to the venerable Gurii: "They call the monks angels in vain—there is no comparison with angels, nor is there a likeness; but they should pattern themselves after the Apostles whom Christ sent to teach and to baptize!"

Kiriak came the next day to give me my lesson and straightway fell at my feet.

"What's the matter? What's the matter?" I said lifting him up. "Good teacher, it's not right for you to bow at the feet of your pupil."

"No, Your Grace, you have already comforted me greatly, comforted me so much that I hadn't hoped for such in this life!"

"And why, man of God," I said, "are you so happy with me?"

"Because you told the monks to learn, and when they go forth it is *first to teach, and then to baptize.* Your Grace, you are right in establishing this order, Christ commanded it and Proverbs teaches it: 'Also, that the soul be without knowledge, it is not good.'[2] They are all able to baptize, but unable to teach the Word."

1 Literally, "ambo."
2 Proverbs 19:2a.

"Well, you really understood me in a wider sense than I intended, it seems," I said. "And according to your understanding children wouldn't have to be baptized."

"Christian children are another matter, Your Grace."

"Well, yes; though Prince Vladimir wouldn't have baptized our forefathers if he had waited long for their education."

But he replied to me, "Eh, Your Grace, you know it really might've been better if they'd taught them first. And maybe you've read in the Chronicles that very soon everything boiled over, 'since Vladimir's piety was mediated by fear.' Metropolitan Platon wisely said, 'Vladimir was hasty, but the Greeks played a cunning trick. They baptized uneducated ignoramuses.' Are we to follow their haste and slyness? You know that they're 'smooth-tongued even to this day.' Thus, we're baptized into Christ, but don't clothe ourselves in Christ. It's futile to baptize this way, Your Grace!"

"How is it futile, Father Kiriak?" I said. "What are you preaching, Father?"

"What then, Your Grace?" he answered. "Hasn't a pious teacher written that baptism of an ignoramus with water alone doesn't serve for the acquisition of eternal life."

I looked at him and said seriously, "Listen, Father Kiriak, you know that you're falling into heresy."

"No, I'm not heretical," he answered. "I'm speaking according to the right belief of Saint Cyril of Jerusalem on the baptismal mysteries: 'Simon the Magician wet his body with water in the font, but his heart was not illumined by the Spirit, his body went down into the water and came up, but his soul was not buried together with Christ, nor with Him raised.' That he was baptized, that he was bathed, made no difference since he wasn't a Christian. The Lord lives and your soul lives, Your Grace. Remember, how it's written: There are those who are baptized who will hear, 'I know you not,'[3] and unbaptized who will justify themselves by works of conscience and enter the Kingdom, since they preserved justice and truth. Is it possible that you reject this?"

3 See Luke 13:23 and following.

Well, I thought, let's wait to talk about this, and said, "Come on, brother, let's study the language of the heathen and not the language of Jerusalem. Take the pointer and don't become terribly angry if I'm not an intelligent pupil."

"I won't be angry, Your Grace," he answered.

The good-natured and outspoken old man was truly remarkable and taught wonderfully. With intelligence and speed he disclosed to me all the secrets of how to understand their speech, which is poor and has so few words that it's hardly possible to call it a language. In any case it's nothing more than a language of animal existence and not of intellectual life; meanwhile, it's very difficult to master. The phrases are short and have no tenses, making it extremely difficult to translate any written text which is generated according to the rules of a developed language—which has complicated tenses and subordinate phrases—into this speech; and poetical and figurative expressions cannot be translated at all, quite understandably since such expressions might remain inaccessible to these poor people. How could you explain to them the meaning of the saying, "Be ye therefore wise as serpents, and harmless as doves,"[4] when they have seen neither snakes nor doves and are unable to imagine them. It's impossible to select words in their language to translate: martyr, baptist, forerunner; but if All-Holy Virgin is translated according to their words *sochmo Abya*, one does not come out with our Mother of God, but some sort of shamanist female deity—briefly, a *goddess*. On the merits of the Holy Blood or of the other sacraments of the faith it is even more difficult to speak; and one couldn't think of constructing some sort of theological system, or simply mentioning a birth from a virgin without a husband. They would either understand nothing of it, which might be best, or very likely laugh right in your face.

Kiriak communicated all of this to me, and communicated it so well that I learned the spirit of the language and understood the whole spirit of this poor people; and what to me was more amusing than anything else was how Kiriak had broken through all my assumed severity in the most unobtrusive manner. We developed a most pleasant relation between us, light and so

4 Matthew 10:16.

jocular, that later maintaining his jocular tone at the completion of all my lessons I ordered a pot of porridge to be prepared, placed a silver ruble on it and some black material for a cassock, and carried all of it personally—like a graduating student—to Kiriak's cell.

He lived under the belltower in such a small cell that when I entered there was hardly room for the two of us to turn around, and the vaults of the ceiling weighed down directly on our heads; but everything here was tidy, even the aster in the broken cooking pot blooming in the dim, grated window.

I found Kiriak at work. He was threading fish scales and sewing them onto a piece of cloth.

"What are you concocting?" I said.

"Little decorations, Your Grace."

"What sort of little decorations?"

"Little decorations for the little native girls. They come to the fair and I give presents away to them."

"So that's how you make the unbelieving heathens happy?"

"Just a minute, Your Grace! You don't really mean all this 'unbelieving this' and 'unbelieving that.' One Lord created all. They should be pitied for they're blind."

"They need to be enlightened, Father Kiriak."

"To enlighten, it's good to enlighten, Your Grace," he said. "Yes, enlighten," —and he started murmuring, "Let your light so shine before men, that they may see your good deeds."[5]

"But here I've come to you with obeisance,"[6] I said, "and brought you a pot of porridge for my tutoring."

"Well, how nice," he said. "Sit down and have some porridge. You'll be my guest."

He seated me on a small stump, he sat on another, then he put my porridge on a bench between us and said, "Well, partake of this with me, Your Grace. Your own good gift I'm pleased to offer you."

So we began to eat, the old man and I, and we got into a conversation.

---

5 Matthew 5:16.
6 Literally, with a *poklon*, meaning "in thanksgiving."

Chapter Five

To tell the truth I was greatly interested in what had induced Kiriak to deviate from his successful missionary activities and had compelled him so strangely—according to the view I held at the time—to be almost criminally negligent toward this work or, in any event, to regard it as a temptation.

"What shall we talk about?" I said. "After a good welcome, a good conversation is in order. Tell me: Do you know how we can teach the Faith to these natives who are continually under your protection?"

"We must teach, Your Grace, teach and show them a good example by our good living."

"And where are you and I to teach them?"

"I don't know, Your Grace. We should go to them to teach."

"That's it then."

"Yes, we need to teach, Your Grace. Both in the morning we must sow the seeds and in the evening we must not give our hand rest. We must continually sow."

"You speak well. Why aren't you doing anything?"

"Pardon me, Your Grace, but don't ask."

"No, you have to tell me."

"If you're demanding that I tell you, then explain: Why should I go there?"

"To teach and to baptize."

"To teach?—I'm incompetent to teach, Your Grace."

"Why? Doesn't the Enemy[1] allow it?"

"No-o! What Enemy—is he such an important person to the baptized. Make the sign of the cross with one finger and he vanishes; but the little enemies interfere. That's the trouble!"

"What are these 'little enemies'?"

1 Satan or the Evil One.

"Clothing sizers, old philanthropizers, commissioners, officeholders, minor officials with red tape."

"Have these become more powerful than the Enemy himself?"

"There can be no question of it. You know, this kind cannot be exorcised, neither by prayer nor fasting."

"Well, you must simply baptize then, as all baptize."

"Baptize..." —Kiriak repeated after me, and suddenly became silent and smiled.

"What is it? Continue."

The smile vanished from Kiriak's face, and he added with a serious, even stern, expression, "No, I don't want to do this as a fast snatch."

"Wha-a-t?"

"I just don't want to do it this way, Your Grace, that's it!" he said firmly and smiled again.

"What are you smiling at?" I said. "And what if I order you to baptize?"

"I won't obey," he answered wearing a good-natured smile; and with a familiar slap on my knee, he continued, "Listen, Your Grace, I don't know if you've read it or not. There's a wonderful story in the *Lives of the Saints*."

But I interrupted and said, "Spare me the *Lives*, please. Here we're speaking of the Word of God and not of legends about people. You monks know that it's possible to get this and that from the *Lives*, and so you love to seize upon all sorts of quotes from them."

But he answered, "Let me finish, Your Grace. Maybe I'll find something applicable from the *Lives*."

And he told an old story from the first Christian centuries about two friends, a Christian and a pagan, the former of whom often talked to the latter about Christianity and continually annoyed him with it; so the pagan, who up until that time had been indifferent, suddenly began to curse and spew out the most malicious blasphemies against Christ and against Christianity, but while he was doing it his horse reared and killed him. The other man, the Christian, saw in this a miracle and was horrified that his friend, the pagan, left this life with such a feeling of animosity toward Christ. The Christian grieved over it and wept bitterly, saying: It would have been much better if I had said nothing to him about Christ, then he wouldn't have gotten irritated at Him and wouldn't have replied as he did. But he was consoled, for it was communicated to him spiritually that his friend was received by Christ, because when no one was pestering the pagan so insistently, he himself had thought about Christ inwardly, and because of this with his last breath he called to Him.

Kiriak said, "And That One was in his heart. He immediately embraced him and gave him a resting place."

"Again, it appears everything is close to the heart."[2]

"Yes, close to the heart."

"Look, Father Kiriak," I said, "your trouble is that you're too much disposed to things close to the heart."

"Ah, Your Grace, and how am I not to be disposed to them. Very great mysteries already go on there. All blessings come from there: mother's milk which nourishes little children, love dwells there, and faith. Believe it. It's so, Your Grace. It's there, everything is there. You can call it forth only with the heart, and not by reason. Reason doesn't create it, but destroys it. Reason brings forth doubts, Your Grace, but faith gives peace, it gives joy...This, I tell you, greatly consoles me. You look to see how things are going and are angry, but I always rejoice."

"What's there to rejoice about?"

"Because everything is very good."

"What's very good?"

"Everything, Your Grace, whatever is revealed to us and whatever is hidden from us. Your Grace, I think that we're all going to one banquet."

"Do me a favor and speak more directly. Do you utterly reject plain, old baptism with water or what?"

"I hardly reject it! Oh, Your Grace, Your Grace! How many years I've been pining for, always waiting for, a person with whom I could talk heart-to-heart, freely about spiritual matters; and having come to know you, I thought that you at last were

2 Literally, "in your bosom."

the one. But now you're picking on my every word like a prosecuting attorney! What do you want? —every word a lie and I as well. I don't reject anything; but you should consider these various attitudes I arrived at—and out of love, not out of hate. Bear with me, and hear me out."

"Fine," I answered, "I'll listen to your sermonizing."

"Well, here we are both baptized—and that's good. It's as if we've been given a ticket to a banquet. We go and we know that we're invited because we have a ticket."

"Well!"

"Well, but now we see alongside us a person without a ticket wandering along in the same direction. We think, 'What a fool! He's going for nothing. They won't let him in! He'll get there and the doorkeepers will turn him away.' And we arrive and observe: The doorkeepers do turn him away because he has no ticket, but the host sees it, and perhaps he'll order them to let him in, saying, 'Never mind that there's no ticket, I know him well. Please, come in.' And he would lead him in, showing him a place of greater honor than some of those who arrived with a ticket."

I said, "Do you instill this in the natives?"

"No. Why would this be instilled in them? I only reason this way within myself, as is suggested by Christ's goodness and wisdom."

"Yes, you understand this; but do you understand His wisdom?"

"How could I, Your Grace! You can't grasp it, but...I'm speaking about what the heart feels. When I must do something, I always ask myself mentally: Can I do this to the glory of Christ? If it's possible, then I do it, but if it's not, then I don't want to do it."

"Then is this your principal catechesis?"[3]

"It's my first and last, Your Grace. Everything is included in it. For simple hearts, Your Grace, it's very handy! You know, it's simple: you can't get drunk on vodka to the glory of Christ; you can't fight or steal to the glory of Christ; you can't leave a person helpless...And the natives soon come to understand and

3 Basic spiritual instruction.

praise it. 'Your little Christ,' they say, 'is good—righteous.' It turns out well according to their understanding."

"That, if you like, is well and good."

"Fair to middlin', Your Grace; but what seems no good to me is how the newly baptized come to the city and see everything that the baptized do there, and they ask: Is it possible to do this to the glory of Christ? What do I answer them, Your Grace? Do Christians or non-Christians live there? To say 'non-Christians'—is shameful, to call them Christians—is a terrible sin."

"How do you answer?"

Kiriak made a gesture of hopelessness and whispered, "I don't say anything, but...I cry."

I understood that his religious morality had come into conflict with a certain kind of "politics." He read Tertullian, "On Public Spectacles," and inferred that "for the glory of Christ" it's impossible to go to the theater, or dance, or play cards, or do many other of the things which contemporary, so-called Christians are unable to do without. He was an innovator of sorts. Seeing the falsity of this world, he was ashamed of it and awaited a new one filled with spirit and truth. When I hinted at this to him, he immediately agreed with me.

"Yes," he said, "yes, these people are of the flesh. But why show the flesh? It needs to be hidden. At least don't let the name of Christ be degraded by them in front of the pagans."

"But why, if what they say is true, are these local natives still coming to you?"

"They trust me and come."

"Yes, precisely. But why?"

"They come when they argue or quarrel. They say to settle it according to the little Christ."

"And then you settle it?"

"Yes, I know their customs. I apply the mind of Christ and say how it should be."

"And then they follow it?"

"They follow it. They love His fairness. At other times the sick or possessed come. They ask for prayers."

"How do you treat the possessed? Do you rebuke the demons or what?"

"No, Your Grace. I pray and comfort them."

"You know their shamans have a reputation for being adept at that."

"That's right, Your Grace, not every shaman is the same. Some really know a great deal about the secret powers of nature. Well, you know, shamans aren't so bad...They know me and some send people to me."

"How did you get on friendly terms with shamans?"

"This is what happened. The Buddhist lamas persecuted them and our officials put many shamanists in prison; but it's very tedious for a nomad to be in prison. God only knows what happened to some of them. Well, I, a sinner, used to visit the prison, and would finagle some goodies for them from the merchants and console them with a good word."

"And then what?"

"They were grateful; they took them in Christ's name and praised Him. He is good, they would say, and kind. And you be quiet, Your Grace, for they themselves don't recognize how they touch the hem of His garment."

"Yes, but how do they touch it?" I said. "You know, all this seems senseless!"

"Your Grace! Why do you always poke your nose in so fast! God's work gets done in its own good time.[4] Weren't there six water pots at the marriage feast in Cana; but you know all of them mustn't have been filled at the same time, but they were full up one after the other. Our Christ, though Himself a great miracle-worker, first spat on the blind Jew's eyes, and then He opened them. And you know that these people are even more blind than the Jew was. How much can we demand of them right now? Let them touch the very hem of His garment. They'll feel His goodness, and He'll snatch them off to Himself."[5]

"Well really, 'snatch them off'!"

"So what?"

"You're using such inappropriate words."

4 Literally,"God's work has its own way, it goes along without bustle."
5 A colloquialism in Russian, as when a wolf "snatches" a sheep.

"But how is it inappropriate, Your Grace—the word is quite simple. He, our benefactor, Himself not descended from boyar lineage, isn't judged for His simplicity. Who could know His generation, for He walked with shepherds, went about with sinners and wasn't squeamish about a mangy sheep; and wherever He found one, He'd pick it up on His holy shoulders and carry it to the Father. Well, but That One...what was He to do? He didn't want to grieve His long-suffering Son. He'll let the slovenly sheep into the sheepfold for His sake."

"Well, good," I said. "You aren't quite suited to be a catechist, Brother Kiriak, however you could prove yourself useful as a baptizer, though a little heretical. In spite of your wishes I'm going to equip you for baptizing."

But Kiriak became terribly agitated and upset. "Be merciful, Your Grace," he said. "Why do you have to force me? Christ will forbid you to do this! And nothing will come of this, nothing, nothing, and nothing!"

"Why is that?"

"It's so, because this door is bolted to us."

"And who locked it?"

"He Who holds the Key of David: 'He that openeth, and no man shutteth; and shutteth, and no man openeth.'[6] Or have you forgotten Revelation?"

"Kiriak," I said, "too many books are making you mad."

"No, Your Grace, I'm not mad; but if you don't listen to me, then you'll hurt people and offend the Holy Spirit, and all you'll do is make church bureaucrats happy, for they'll be able to brag and tell more lies in their accountings."

I stopped listening to him; however, I didn't abandon the idea of changing his current, capricious attitude and of sending him out for sure. But what do you think happened? You know, not only simple-hearted Amos of the Old Testament, who used to gather berries, suddenly began to prophesy; but my Kiriak prophesied to me, and his words, "and Christ will forbid it," began to come true. At the same time, as luck would have it, I received a notice from officials in Petersburg that, according to

6 Revelation 3:7. Although the book is considered Scripture, it is not read liturgically in the Orthodox Church.

their governmental supervision, they were increasing the number of Buddhist temples for those of us in Siberia and doubling the staff of lamas. Though I was born on Russian soil and had learned not to be surprised at anything unexpected, still I confess that this order *contra jus et fas*[7] made me dumb-struck; but what was worse, it totally bewildered those poor, newly-baptized. What was perhaps more pitiful, it bewildered the worthy missionaries. News of these joyful events to the detriment of Christianity and to the benefit of Buddhism spread through the entire region like the wind. To disseminate the news horses ran, reindeer ran, dogs ran, and Siberia was informed that "the all-powerful and all-victorious" god Fo[8] had "overpowered and gained victory over the little Christ" in Petersburg. The lamas in their jubilation assured everyone that our highest ranking officials and our Dalai Lama himself, that is the Metropolitan of Moscow, had embraced Buddhism. Hearing news of this, the missionaries became frightened. They didn't know what they should do. It seems some of them rather had their doubts: To be sure, things in Petersburg could have changed to the side of the lamas, as they turned to Catholicism at another subtle and intriguing time, and things turn to spiritualism, even now in our well-thought-out but foolish days. Only today, it stands to reason, it's happening more quietly, because although now the chosen idol is frail, now also no one is inclined to kick against this goad.[9] But at that time this cold-blooded self-control was missing from many, and I, a sinner, was in that number. I could not look with indifference on my poor baptizers who trudged back to me for safety from the steppes *on foot*. Not one of them in the whole district had a nag or a reindeer or a dog; and God only knows how they got through snowdrifts on foot and arrived torn-up and dirty, certainly not appearing like priests of God Almighty, but like cripples and beggars. The officials and the whole of the regular administration protected the lamas without a twinge of conscience. It was my responsibility to spar with the governor so that he, a Christian boyar, would restrain his sub-

7 Latin, "contrary to justice and right".
8 A name used of Buddha which is associated with overcoming the seductive falsities of the world and other temptations.
9 The phrase is from Acts 9:5.

ordinates, however little, in order that they at least would not openly render assistance to Buddhism. The governor, as usual, took offense, and a brutal engagement ensued. I complained to him about his staff, while he wrote to me about my missionaries, that "no one bothers them, though they themselves are lazy and inept." But my deserting missionaries, in their turn, squealed that although no one exactly gagged their mouths, no one anywhere would give them a horse or a reindeer because everyone everywhere on the steppes was afraid of the lamas. "The lamas are rich," they say, "they give money to the officials, but we have no money for this purpose."

What could I say to comfort them? I could have promised to present a proposal to the Synod that the lauras[10] and monasteries possessing "much wealth" would share with us in our poverty and allow us some such sum with which we could bribe officials; but I was afraid that in the great halls of the Synod they would consider that this good was inappropriate, and praying to God, very likely refuse me aid for bribery. Nonetheless, even if we did get it, this remedy might prove hopeless in our hands. My apostles revealed such a weakness in themselves which, in conjunction with the situation, took on a very important significance.

They said, "We were seized by pity for the savages. This trouble is going to knock them senseless. Today we baptize them, tomorrow the lamas reconvert them and order them to deny Christ, and take their possessions from them as a penalty. The poor people become more impoverished of their livestock and of their scant understanding—their understanding mixes up all faiths, is lame in both legs, but they complain to us."

Kiriak was very interested in this struggle, and enjoying my good favor, often stopped me with a question: "What have your little enemies written to you, Your Grace?" or "What have you written to your little enemies, Your Grace?" Once he even appeared with a request: "Your Grace, would you consult with me when you'll be writing to the little enemies?"

10 "lauras" or "lavras": This type of monastery is a very ancient one wherein a number of monks live a communal life, yet inhabit separate cells grouped around a church.

This was the occasion when the governor reproved me with the fact that in the neighboring diocese under identical circumstances to those in which I found myself, preaching and baptizing were being performed successfully; and he pointed out to me a certain missionary named Peter, a Zyryan,[11] who baptized whole masses of natives.

Such a circumstance baffled me, and I asked the neighboring bishop is it so? He answered that it really was, that he had a Zyryan, Father Peter, who twice went to preach and the first time "all the baptismal crosses were used up," but the second time he took twice as many crosses and again there weren't enough—so he successively hung one cross on one neck and then another.

When Kiriak heard this he lamented greatly. "My God," he said, "where did this insidious master come from to add to all our troubles? He'll drown Christ, in His own Church and in His own Blood! Oh, what a shame! Be merciful, Your Grace. Quickly ask the bishop to stop this servant of the Faith, that at least enough strength may be left in the Church for future planting."

"Father Kiriak, you're talking nonsense," I said. "Can I restrain someone from such praiseworthy zeal?"

He implored me, "Oh yes, Your Grace, ask him. You don't understand about this, but I know the significance of what's going on now in the steppes. This isn't all for Christ, but the service he's doing there is for the little enemies. Him they will drown, they will drown our little dove in blood, and they'll scare the people away from Him for the next hundred years."

I didn't listen to Kiriak, to be sure; but on the contrary, I wrote to the neighboring bishop so that he would lend me his Zyryan, or as the Siberian aristocrats say in French, *au proka*.[12] By this time my neighbor, the bishop, had already served out his term, moved to Russia and did not support keeping his idle baptizer. The Zyryan was sent to me, so great-bearded, garrulous, and as they say, greasy from head to toe. I immediately

11 See the Translator's Preface for a description of the Zyryans.
12 This expression is a mixture of French and Russian meaning "on loan" or "for hire." (The Russian word *naprokat* has been given an affected, French veneer.)

sent him to the steppes, and within a couple of weeks I already received good news. He informed me that he was baptizing people right and left. He only had one fear: Would he have enough crosses, though he had taken a pretty good-sized box? From this I could unmistakenly conclude that the catch in the net of this lucky fisherman was extraordinarily plentiful.

Now, I thought, I've finally found for myself a real master for the job! And I was very glad about it, glad indeed! I shall tell you openly why, from a very bureaucratic point of view, because...gentlemen, a bishop is only human, and he becomes overburdened when one authority comes along with, "Baptize," but another with, "Leave it alone." Well, quite! It soon would be settled in one way, and since I came across the adroit baptizer, let him baptize the whole lot, and maybe then people will be happier.

But Kiriak didn't share my view, and one evening when I was coming out of the bathhouse he met me. He stopped and greeted me, "Hello, Your Grace!"

"Hello, Father Kiriak," I said.

"Did you wash well?"

"Yes."

"Did you wash off the Zyryan?"

I got angry. "What's this foolishness?" I said.

He went on again about the Zyryan. "He's merciless," he said. "Now he's baptizing among our people the way he did beyond Lake Baikal. By it those he baptizes are only made to suffer, but they complain of Christ. It's a sin for you all, but you have the greater sin, Your Grace!"

I considered Kiriak crude, but all the same I took his words to heart. What's one to think? You know, he's basically a solid fellow, he's not just drivelling away. Wherein lies the secret? How does the adroit Zyryan whom I took "on loan" really baptize? I had a notion of the religiosity of the Zyryans. For the most part they are church-builders, their icons everywhere are excellent and even rich; but of all the peoples in the world calling themselves Christians, it must be confessed, they're the most superficial. No one better fits the definition that, "They have God in their churches, but not in their hearts."[13] But did

13 Literally,"God is only in their icons, but not in their inner convictions."

this Zyryan burn the natives with fire so that they would be baptized? That couldn't be! What was going on here? Why was the Zyryan successful but the Russians weren't, and up to that moment I still didn't know why?

Then the thought came to me, "But all of this is because you, Your Grace, and those like you are egotistical and pompous. You collect 'much money,' and only drive about under ringing church bells, but you think little about the far reaches of your pastorate and you pass judgment thereon by rumor. You complain of your powerlessness in your own country, while reaching for the stars and asking, 'What will you give me if I deliver Him to you?'[14] Have you been careful, brother, that you haven't become like this?"

That evening I paced back and forth in my empty, dull quarters with these thoughts until I reached the moment when the idea suddenly came to me: I myself must pass through the wilderness. In this way I hoped to size up for myself, if not all, then most of, the situation. And I confess to you, I thought it would be refreshing.

Due to my inexperience and in order to properly conduct this foray, I needed a person who knew the native language well; but who would one wish for better than Kiriak? And in accord with my impatience I didn't put it off, but summoned Kiriak, revealed my plan to him and ordered him to get ready.

He didn't gainsay me, but on the contrary appeared to be very happy, and repeated while smiling, "With God's help! With God's help!"

There was no need to delay, so very early the next morning we sang the Liturgy, both put on native dress and left, taking the road straight north where my Zyryan carried on his apostolic mission.

14 He quotes the words of Judas in betraying Jesus in Matthew 26:15.

Chapter Six

The first day we dashed along in a fine troika[1] and Father Kiriak and I conversed the whole while. The amiable old man told me interesting stories from the religious traditions of the natives. Among them the tale I found particularly engaging was about five hundred travelers who set out to journey the world under the leadership of a certain man of learning they called *Obushy* or Book-man. It was still during a time when the god Shigemuny[2] "was conquering the demonic powers and overcoming all weakness" and was feasting with guests on the "never-ending banquet" in Shirvas. This legend is especially interesting because in it one can feel the whole spirit and mentality of this people's religious imagination. Five hundred wayfarers, led by Book-man, meet a ghost which takes on the most horrible and abominable appearance in order to frighten them, and it asks, "Do you have monsters like this?"

"We have much worse," Book-man answered.

"Who are they?"

"All those who are envious, greedy, lying, and vindictive. When death takes them they become monsters more terrible and vile than you are."

The ghost hid itself, somewhere changed into a man so dried-up and gaunt that his veins seemed glued to his bones, appeared again before the wayfarers and said, "Do you have people like this?"

"We have people more dried-up than you," answered Bookman. "All such seek honors."

"Hm!" I interrupted Kiriak. "Watch out, doesn't the greater moral of this story refer to us bishops?"

1 A sleigh drawn by three horses abreast.

2 *Sakyamuni*, the Sanskrit epithet referring to Gautama Buddha, means "sage of the Sakya tribe."

"God only knows, Your Grace," and he continued. "In a little while the ghost appeared in the form of a handsome youth and said, 'Do you have people like this?' 'Of course,' Book-man answered, 'among us are those incomparably handsomer than you. They are those who have keen understanding and, having cleansed their passions, revere three graces: God, faith, and holiness. These are so much handsomer than you that you pale by comparison.' The ghost got mad and began to test Book-man in other ways. He cupped his hand and scooped up some water. 'Where is there more water,' he said, 'in the sea or in my hand?' 'In your hand,' Book-man answered. 'Prove it.' 'All right, I'll prove it. Judging by appearances, there really seems to be more water in the sea than in your hand; but when the time comes for the destruction of the world, and another, brighter-burning sun comes from the purest one and dries up all the waters in the world—both the great and the small seas and the rivers and the streams, and Soumber Mountain (Atlas)[3] itself crumbles—whoever has wet the lips of the thirsty with his hand during this life or has washed the wounds of the poor with his hand, for that one seven suns won't dry up his handful of water, but just the opposite, will expand and increase it.'"

"...All right, as you like, but isn't this just a bit stupid, gentlemen?" our narrator, the Archbishop, interrupted himself, stopping for a minute. "—Well? No, what do you really think of it?"

"It's not stupid, Your Eminence, it's not stupid at all."

I must confess to you, it seemed to me a bit more sensible than some lengthy sermons on justification...Well, it's not about that anyhow. Later on we got into long discussions about which is the most preferable method for converting the natives to Christianity. Kiriak found that it was best to have as little religious ceremony with them as possible, or else they would surpass Kirik himself with questions about it, such as: "Is it possible to commune someone who taps his teeth with an egg?" And it's unnecessary to teach much dogma because their weak intellects get tired following every abstraction and syllogism, but it's best to talk

3 Usually spelled "Sumer," this high primordial mountain of Buddhist cosmology (cf. Olympus) is to be destroyed, along with its gifted inhabitants, by five suns at the destruction of the present world.

actions speak louder than words

simply to them about the life and miracles of Christ, so that it would appear to them as much as possible a living image, and so that their poor imagination would be able to catch onto something. But most important, he always emphasized this, "Whoever is wise and skillful,[4] let him show them by his good life, then they'll catch the meaning of Christ, but otherwise," he said, "what we're doing is bad. Although our faith is true, and we talk about it among them, it'll be subordinated to their untrue faith. Ours'll only be passive, but theirs'll be active— what's the good in that, Your Grace?"

"Consider: Will it be for the glory of the Christian religion or its humiliation? What's still more painful is that they'd take something from us, not knowing what to do with it. There's no need to hurry to say it, but it's necessary to plant it. Others'll come, they'll tend it, but God Himself gives the growth. Isn't it so, Your Grace, what the apostle taught? Call him to mind, it must be so. See that we don't rush, so people won't mock and Satan won't be glad." *religion w/out bureacracy*

To tell the truth I inwardly agreed with him for the most part, and didn't notice how the day passed to evening in simple and peaceful conversation with him; but at the same time our trip by horse-drawn sleigh ended.

We both spent the night by the fire in a yurt[5] and on the next morning embarked on a reindeer sleigh.

The weather was excellent and traveling by reindeer interested me very much, though it wasn't quite as I had imagined. In my childhood I very much liked to look at a print in which there was a Laplander in his reindeer sleigh. But the reindeer in the print were light, swift-footed, and flew like the wind across the steppes, throwing back their branch-antlered heads. And I always used to think, "Oh, if only once I could ride like this! How great the speed at a gallop!" But the reality was much different. Before me were not those antlered whirlwinds that would carry us off, but camel-like, rather heavy louts with hanging heads and pulpy, splayed hoofs. They ran with an unsteady and rough gait, heads bent low, and with such heavy breathing that anyone not used to it felt sorry to look at them,

4 The expression is Church Slavic and antiquated.
5 A light, movable tent used by Siberian nomads.

especially when their nostrils were frozen over and their mouths
were agape. Their breathing was so labored that their breath
formed a dense cloud which hung like a stripe behind us in the
frozen air. And this travel and the melancholy monotony of the
deserted scenery which opened before us produced such a tedious impression that we didn't feel like talking; and while
going two days by reindeer Kiriak and I hardly conversed at all.

On the evening of the third day this type of travel ended.
The snow became more powdery and we exchanged the clumsy
reindeer for dogs—as gray, shaggy, and sharp-eared as little
wolves, and they almost yelped like wolves. They harness them
in great numbers, about fifteen apiece, and perhaps they would
hook up more for an honored traveler; but the dogsleds are so
narrow that it's impossible for two people to sit side by side, so
that Father Kiriak and I were forced to separate. I had to ride on
one with a driver, and on the other sled rode Kiriak with another
driver. Both drivers seemed equally competent; you couldn't
even distinguish one from the other by their appearance—particularly when they wrapped themselves up in their reindeer-
skin coats, exactly like two slivers of bath soap, both were
equally handsome. But Kiriak found a difference between them
and staunchly insisted that I ride with the one he considered
more trustworthy; but how he sensed this trustworthiness, he
didn't explain.

"It's so, Your Grace" he said. "You're less experienced
than me in these parts, so you ride with him." I didn't listen to
him and sat with the other one. We divided our baggage. I took
a small bundle with linen and books at my feet, while Kiriak
hung the Chrism and Holy Communion kits from his neck and
took at his feet a bag of meal, dried fish, and the rest of our
simple provisions for the journey. Tucked in by reindeer fur, we
settled into the sleds, buttoned reindeer skins onto the top of the
sled down to our knees, and sped off.

The dogsled was much faster than the reindeer sled, but in
return was so uncomfortable (and I was unaccustomed to it) that
within an hour my back felt as though it would break. I glanced
over at Kiriak—he sat straight as a post, but I bounced from side
to side. I always wanted to maintain my balance, and because of
these gymnastics I wasn't even able to talk with my driver. The

only thing I knew was that he was baptized and had been baptized not long ago by my Zyryan, but I couldn't successfully examine him. By evening I was so exhausted that I couldn't hold on any longer and complained to Kiriak.

"I feel terrible," I said. "Something shook me up right from the very beginning."

"It's all because you didn't listen to me," he answered. "You didn't ride with the one I put you with. He drives better, more comfortably. Be kind. Tomorrow switch with me."

"All right," I said, "if you want I'll switch." And I did exactly that and we set out again.

I don't know. Whether I got used to holding my place on that bed of nails from the previous day's ride or whether this driver really handled the rig better, it was more comfortable for me to ride and I could even carry on a conversation.

I asked him whether he was baptized or not.

"No, Fodder,"[6] he answered, "me unbaptized, me lucky."

"Why are you so lucky?"

"Lucky, Fodder. Dzol-Dzayagachy give me, Fodder. She, Fodder, take care me."

Dzol-Dzayagachy is a goddess of the shamanists who grants children and protects the health and happiness of those who address supplications to her.

"Be that as it may," I said, "still why won't you get baptized?"

"But she won't give me up to be baptized, Fodder."

"Who won't? Dzol-Dzayagachy?"

"Yes, Fodder, she won't."

"Ah, well, it's good that you told me."

"Fodder, what's good about it?"

"Because I'll order you to be baptized to spite Dzol-Dzayagachy."

"What you doing, Fodder? Why anger Dzol-Dzayagachy? She'll get mad. She'll start it a-blowing."

6 *Bachka* in Russian, an impossible corruption of the language, is as mistaken as calling a bishop "Father" in English with the mispronunciation "Fodder."

"What do I care about your Dzol-Dzayagachy. I'll baptize you, and that's all there is to it."

"No, Fodder, she won't let me be hurt."

✳ "What's hurtful to you about it, stupid?"

"When you baptize me, Fodder? Me much hurt, Fodder. Zaysan[7] comes—he'll beat me because baptized, shaman comes—he'll beat again, lama comes—he'll also beat and drive off reindeer. I'll be big hurt, Fodder."

"They wouldn't dare do it."

"How won't they dare, Fodder? They dare, Fodder, they take everything. I have an uncle, Fodder, they already ruined...How they ruined him, Fodder, and they ruined my brother, Fodder."

"Do you have a brother who is baptized?"

"Yes, Fodder, I have, I have a brother, Fodder."

"And is he baptized?"

"Yes, Fodder, he's baptized, he's baptized twice."[8]

"What do you mean? Baptized twice? Do they baptize twice?"

"Yes, Fodder, they do."

"You're lying!"

"No, Fodder, it's twice. He got baptized once for himself and once for me, Fodder."

"How for you? What kind of nonsense are you talking about?"

"This nonsense, Fodder! No nonsense. I hid myself from the priest, Fodder, but my brother got baptized in my place."

"Why did you two pull such a trick?"

"Because, Fodder, he's kind."

"Who is, your brother or what?"

"Yes, Fodder, my brother. He said, 'I'm already stuck—baptized—but you hide. I'll be baptized again.' So I hid."

"And where is your brother now?"

"He's run off to be baptized again, Fodder."

7 A local native chief or elder recognized as an official by the tsarist government, in Russian *starshina*.

8 Only one baptism is permitted in the Orthodox Church.

"Where is the bum off to now?"

"To a place where we heard there's a strong priest traveling, Fodder."

"How d'you like that! What's he got to do with this priest?"

"Well, our people are there, Fodder, our people live there, Fodder, good people. So what? He feels sorry, Fodder...he pities them, Fodder, so he ran off to be baptized for them."

"And what kind of shaitan[9] is your brother anyway? How can he dare do this?"

"But why not, Fodder? It's nothing. It's already all the same for him, Fodder, but for them, Fodder, the Zaysan won't beat them and the lama won't drive off their reindeer."

"Hm! However, I'll have to keep an eye on your idle brother. Tell me, what's his name?"

"Kozmo-Demi, Fodder."

"Cosmas or Damian?"[10]

"No, Fodder, Kozmo-Demi."

"Yes. To you it would be clearer: Kozmo-Demi or a copper penny[11]—only they're two names."

"No, Fodder, one."

"I told you—two!"

"No, Fodder, one."

"Well, it's obvious you know better than I."

"Yes, Fodder, I do."

"But did they give him the names Cosmas and Damian at his first or second baptism?"

He looked at me wide-eyed and didn't understand; but when I repeated myself he thought about it and answered, "Yes, Fodder. It was when he was baptized in my place that they began to tease him with Kozmo-Demi."

"But what name did you tease him with after his first baptism?"

"Don't know, Fodder. I forgot."

"But he must know it, mustn't he?"

9 An evil spirit, a rebellious jinn which leads people astray.
10 Only one name is given at baptism in the Orthodox Church.
11 A Russian jingle.

"No, Fodder, he forgot about it."

"That's impossible!" I said.

"No, Fodder, it's true, he forgot about it."

"Well, I'll order to have him found and I'll question him."

"Find him, Fodder, find him, and he'll say that he forgot about it."

"Only when I find him, brother, I'll personally turn him over to the Zaysan."

"It doesn't matter, Fodder. Nothing makes any difference to him now, Fodder. He's hopeless."

"What is it that makes him hopeless? Is it that he was baptized, is that it?"

"Yes, Fodder. The shaman drives him away, the lama took away his reindeer, none of his people trust him."

"Why don't they trust him?"

"Can't trust someone who is baptized, Fodder. No one does."

"You're lying, you foolish savage! Why can't you trust someone who is baptized? Are the baptized worse than you idolaters?"

"Why worse, Fodder? We're all human."

"Do you now agree that he's not worse?"

"I don't know, Fodder. You say he's not worse and I do too; but he can't be trusted."

"Why can't he be trusted?"

"Because, Fodder, the priest forgives him his sins."

"Well, what's wrong with that? Is it really better to remain unforgiven?"

"Fodder, how can anyone stay unforgiven! It's impossible, Fodder. You must ask for forgiveness."

"Well, then I don't understand you. What are you trying to say?"

"This is it, Fodder: The baptized person can steal and tell the priest, then the priest forgives him, Fodder; because of that he's considered untrustworthy by the people, Fodder."

"How d'you like that—what nonsense! But according to you this most likely won't do."

"Fodder, for us this doesn't do, it just doesn't do."

"Well, then how should it be according to all you?"

"Like this, Fodder: If you steal something from someone, you have to take it back and ask forgiveness; the person forgives and God forgives."

"Yes, you see, the priest is a person. Why can't he do the forgiving?"

"Why can't he do the forgiving, Fodder? —The priest can. If someone steals something from the priest, Fodder, then why can't the priest do the forgiving?"

"But if it's stolen from someone else, then the priest can't do the forgiving?"

"How could he, Fodder? It's impossible, Fodder. It wouldn't be right, Fodder. Untrustworthy people would be everywhere, Fodder."

And I thought to myself, "Oh, what an unwashed buffoon you are, what arguments you've constructed for yourself!" And I questioned him further, "But have you heard anything about our Lord, Jesus Christ?"

"Of course, Fodder, I heard."

"What did you hear about Him?"

"He walked on water, Fodder."

"Hm! Well, fine—He walked on water; but what else?"

"Pigs, Fodder, He drowned in the sea."

"And any more than that?"

"Nothing, Fodder. He was good, compassionate, Fodder."

"Well, how was He compassionate? What did He do?"

"He spat in the blind man's eyes, Fodder, the blind man could see. He fed the peoples with loaves and little fish."

"You don't say, brother, you know quite a bit."

"Of course, Fodder, I know quite a bit."

"Who told you all this?"

"People talk about it, Fodder."

"Your people?"

"Which people? Ours, of course, Fodder, ours."

"But from whom did you hear it?"

"Don't know, Fodder."

"Well, don't you know why Christ came here to earth?"

He thought and thought—and he didn't answer.

"Don't you know?" I said.

"Don't know."

I explained the entire Orthodox Faith to him, whether he was listening or not, though the whole time he was whooping at the dogs and brandishing his stick.[12]

"Well," I asked, "did you understand what I've been telling you?"

"Of course, Fodder, I understand: Pigs He drowned in the sea; He spat in the blind man's eyes—the blind man could see; He gave the peoples loaves and little fish."

These swine, the blind man and the little fish stuck in his mind, but nothing else penetrated...I called to mind Kiriak's words about their poor intellect and about how they themselves do not notice they touch the hem of His garment. What then? This one possibly touched the hem, but only just touched it— just barely touched it; but what more could he be given to learn to grasp it firmly? So I tried to talk with him in a simpler way about the blessing of Christ's example and about the reason for His suffering, but at all times my listener continued to brandish his stick imperturbably. It was hard for me to labor under a delusion. I could see that he didn't understand any of it.

"Did you understand anything?" I asked.

"Nothing, Fodder. All your lies are true. I'm sorry for Him. He is good, the little Christ."

"Good?"

"Good, Fodder, we shouldn't hurt Him."

"So you might love Him?"

"How couldn't I love Him, Fodder?"

"What? You can love Him?"

"Of course, Fodder, I've always loved Him, Fodder."

"Well, you're an excellent fellow."

"Thanks, Fodder."

"Now then, all that's left is for you to be baptized. He'll save you."

The native became silent.

12 The stick or *orstel* is an all-purpose, long pole used to drive the dogs (like a whip), to balance the sled, to test the snow, etc.

"What is it, friend?" I said. "Why did you stop talking?"

"No, Fodder."

"What's this 'No, Fodder'?"

"He won't save me, Fodder. Because of Him the Zaysan'll beat me, the shaman'll beat me, the lama'll drive off my reindeer."

"Yes. Here's the real trouble!"

"The trouble, Fodder."

"But you should endure trouble for Christ's sake."

"Why, Fodder, He's compassionate, Fodder. When I croak He Himself will feel sorry for me. Why hurt Him!"

I had intentions of telling him that if he believes that Christ has compassion on him, he should also believe that He could save him; but I restrained myself so as not to hear about the Zaysan and the lama again. It was evident that in the estimation of this man Christ was one of the kind or even the kindest of the deities, but not one of the powerful ones: kind and not powerful. He doesn't stand up for you. He doesn't defend you from the Zaysan or the lama. What could one do here? How could I change his mind when there was no one to back up Christ's side, but there was great support on the other side? A Catholic priest in such a circumstance might use cunning, as they did in China. He might lay a cross at the feet of Buddha and bow down before it, thus assimilating Christ and Buddha, and might boast of his success; but another innovator might give an explanation of Christ in such a way that one need not believe in Him, but merely...think of Him in a seemly manner—and then you'll be all right. But here it was difficult. How could this excellent fellow begin to deliberate, when his entire thinking-mechanism had frozen solid into a lump and he had no way to thaw it out.

It reminded me how superbly Karl Eckartshausen was able with the simplest comparisons to introduce simple people to the magnitude of the sacrifice of Christ's advent on earth, by comparing it to a person who is free, out of love for imprisoned criminals, himself being imprisoned with them in order to share their evil ways. It's very simple and good. But my listener, thanks to the circumstances, knew no greater criminals than those from whom he was running in fear so that they wouldn't baptize him. He had no such place which produced terror in

comparison with the place he customarily lived...You couldn't
do anything with him, not with the works of Massillon or
Bourdaloue or Eckartshausen. There he was, poking his stick
into the snow and waving it, a sliver of bath soap—voicing
nothing. In his peepers, which it would be a shame to call eyes,
not a glimmer of the light of the soul could be found. The
sounds of words themselves which issued from his larynx were
somehow dead. Both in sorrow and in joy, there was always one
pronunciation, languid and passionless. Half the words were
uttered in his gullet and half were squeezed through his teeth.
Where could he search for abstract truths with these means and
what would they mean to him? They would be a burden to him.
He would have to become extinct with his whole race, as the
Aztecs became extinct, as the Native Americans are becoming
extinct...A terrible law! How fortunate that he doesn't know
it—but knows how to poke his stick about in the snow. He
pokes it on the right, he pokes it on the left. He doesn't know
where he's rushing me, why he's rushing, or why he's revealing
to me, like a simple-hearted child, his innermost secrets to his
own harm...He has little talent and...it's a blessing for him, for
little will be asked of him...But he continues to rush along, rush
along into the boundless distance, and brandishes his stick
which flickered before my eyes, and began to affect me like a
pendulum. It loomed before me. Those measured strokes, like
mesmerizing passes, entangled me in their sleepy mesh; drows-
iness invaded my consciousness, and I quietly fell asleep. I fell
asleep only to awaken in a situation from which the Lord should
preserve every living soul!

Chapter Seven

I slept very soundly and probably long enough, but suddenly it seemed as if something pushed me and I sat leaning on my side. Though half asleep I still wanted to right myself, but felt that someone forced me back again. While round about there was continual howling...What happened? I wanted to look, but had nothing to look with—my eyes wouldn't open. I called out to my native. "Hey, you, friend! Where are you?"

But he shouted right into my ear, "Wake up, Fodder, hurry up and wake up! You'll freeze!"

"What happened?" I said, "I can't open my eyes?"

"Right away, Fodder, you'll open them."

And with these words—what do you think?—he went and spat in my eyes, and began rubbing them with the sleeve of his reindeer coat.

"What are you doing?"

"I'm trying to open your eyes, Fodder."

"Get out of here you fool...."

"No, wait a second, Fodder, I'm no fool; so you'll begin to see right away."

And so it was, when he passed his reindeer coat sleeve over my face, my frozen eyelids thawed and opened. But for what? What was there to see? I don't know, maybe it's more terrible in hell. The shadows all around were impermeable, pitch-dark—and they all seemed alive. They quaked and shook like a monster. A solid mass of icy dust was his body, his breath, life-stopping cold. Yes, this was death in one of its most menacing forms, and meeting it face to face, I was terrified.

All that I was able to utter was a question about Kiriak, Where was he? But it was so hard to communicate that the native didn't hear anything. Then I noticed that when speaking to me he stooped down and yelled right into my ear under my ear flap, so I did the same to him. "Where's our other sled?"

"Don't know, Fodder. We broke up."

"How did we break up?"

"We broke up, Fodder."

I didn't want to believe this. I wanted to look back and see them, but nowhere, not in any direction, could anything be seen. Around us was impenetrable hell. Right near my side of the sled something like a ball thronged together, but there wasn't any way to see what it was. I asked the native what it could be.

He answered, "It's the dogs tangled up, Fodder. They're warming themselves." After that he moved about in the darkness and said, "Fall down, Fodder!"

"Where should I fall down?"

"Right here, Fodder. Fall down in the snow."

"Wait a minute," I said. I still couldn't believe that I had lost our Kiriak, and I raised up from the sled and wanted to call him; but at that moment I was smothered, as if choked by the icy dust, and I plopped down in the snow, hitting my head very hard on the bed of the sled. I didn't have any strength to get up, and my native guide wouldn't have let me.

He held me down and said, "Lie down, Fodder, lie still, you won't croak. The snow'll cover us and it'll be warm. Otherwise you'll croak. Lie down!"

There wasn't anything to do except obey him; so I lay down and didn't budge, while he pulled a reindeer skin off the sled, threw it over me and crawled under it himself.

"There now, Fodder," he said, "it's gonna be nice."

But this "nice" was so bad smelling that I had to immediately turn my face as far in the opposite direction from my neighbor as possible, for his presence in close quarters was unbearable. Lazarus dead four days in the tomb in Bethany couldn't smell more foul than this living man. It was something worse than a corpse. It was a combination of the stink of reindeer hide, acrid human sweat, soot and damp rot, *iukola*,[1] fish oil, and filth...Oh, God, oh, poor me! How could I be so repulsed by this, my brother, created in Your image! Oh, how I

1 Fish dried in the air, possibly of a type used as food for the dog teams.

would gladly rush out of this stinking grave in which he placed me next to himself, if only I would have the might and main to withstand this hellish, swirling chaos! But nothing similar to such a possibility could be expected—so I had to resign myself.

My native noticed that I turned away from him and said, "Wait, Fodder, you put your mug[2] in the wrong place. You should put your mug over here, we'll blow at each other. It'll get warmer."

It even seemed to sound terrible! I pretended that I didn't hear him, but he suddenly rolled over me like a bedbug and lay nose to nose, and began breathing in my face with terrible glanders and stench. His respiration was also extraordinary, like a blacksmith's bellows. I could in no way endure this and resolved to change it so that it would stop.

"Breathe a little softer," I said.

"But why? It doesn't matter, Fodder, I'm not tired. I'm warming your mug, Fodder."

To be sure, I didn't take umbrage at his use of the word "mug" because I didn't have any pride at the moment, and what's more, I'll repeat that they consider such a nuance an unnecessary subtlety—distinguishing between a beast's snout and a human face. Separate words still haven't been established. Everything is a mug: he himself has a mug; his wife has a mug; his reindeer has a mug; and his god Shigemuny has a mug. Why shouldn't the bishop have a mug? It was easy for my reverence to put up with this, but what was hard: To put up with his breath smelling of dried fish and some other repulsive stench—probably the stench of his own stomach. I couldn't stand it.

"Enough, stop," I said. "You've warmed me, now don't blow at me anymore."

"No, Fodder, we must—it'll be warmer."

"No, please, it's unnecessary, and it's tiresome. It's unnecessary!"

"Well, we don't have to, Fodder, we don't have to. Now we'll go to sleep."

"Go to sleep."

2 Literally, a "snout" in Russian.

"You go to sleep too, Fodder."

And in the very instant when the words left his mouth, like a well-trained horse that can immediately break into a gallop, he too immediately fell asleep and immediately began to snore. And how the rascal snored! I must confess to you that since childhood I have felt terrible enmity toward those who snore in their sleep, and if there is one person snoring in a room, I become a martyr and can't fall asleep for anything; and so it was at our seminary and academy where, of course, there were many snorers. Though much against my will, I listened to them attentively, so that it can be said in all seriousness that I have made some observations about their snoring: I assure you that one can judge the temperament and character of a person by his snoring, the same as by his voice or by his walk. I assure you that it's so. A feisty person snores passionately as if becoming angry in his sleep. A friend of mine at the academy was jovial and a dandy, so he snored dandily, so jovially, with a whistle, as if he were going to his town cathedral wearing the last word in gentlemen's apparel.[3] People even used to come from other dormitories to listen to him and admire his art. But my present neighbor, the native, conducted such unbelievable music, I have never observed or heard such an extensive range or such a tempo. It was as if a thick, powerful swarm of bees buzzed, and in their humming softly throbbed against the walls of a dry behive. And thus it was wonderful, solid, rhythmical, and measured, oo-oo-oo-bum, bum, bum, oo-oo-oo-bum, bum, bum...According to such observations, it might be incumbent to conclude that this results from a man thorough and trustworthy; but the cold, hard fact was that I didn't get to the point of making an observation. The brigand quite overpowered me with the din! I suffered—suffered long, and in the end could not endure. I poked him in the ribs. "Don't snore," I said.

"How come, Fodder? Why not snore?"

"Because you snore horribly. I can't get any sleep."

"Then you should snore too."

"But I don't know how to snore."

3 Literally, a frock coat.

"But I do, Fodder." And with that he was off again at a gallop, droning away.

What could you do with such an artist? How could you argue with someone who excels in everything? He knows more than I about baptism, about how many times one could be baptized; he is well-versed about names, and he knows how to snore, which I do not. He has the advantage over me in everything. He should be duly honored, and given his stead.

I drew back away from him as far as I could and a little to the side, with difficulty got my hand into my inner cassock and pressed the button on my watch. The watch struck only 3:45. This meant it was still daytime; of course, the snow storm would continue all night and perhaps longer...Siberian blizzards last a long, long time. Can you imagine how it was to have all this before you! In the meantime, my predicament was worsening. On top we were certainly well-covered with snow and in our den it was not only warm, but even stifling; and with that, horrible, stinking fumes were getting thicker. From this suffocating stench I couldn't get my breath and it was a pity that it hadn't happened right away, because then I wouldn't have experienced one one-hundredth part of these sufferings, which I felt when I recalled that my water fortified with cognac and all our provisions were lost with Father Kiriak...I saw clearly that if I didn't suffocate here, as if in the Black Hole of Calcutta, then I was probably in danger of the most horrible, most painful of all deaths: death from hunger and thirst—which had already started to torment me. Oh, how I now regretted that I didn't remain above to freeze, but crawled into this snowy casket where the two of us were lying, so close together and under such weight that all my effort to raise myself up and stand were absolutely futile!

With the greatest difficulty I could get pieces of snow from under my shoulder and gulped them down one after the other, but, alas, it didn't help me a bit. On the contrary, it caused me to be nauseous and brought on an unbearable burning in my throat and stomach, especially around my heart. The back of my head was splitting, my ears were ringing, and the pressure on my eyes was pushing them out of their sockets. While all the time the tiresome swarm of bees buzzed louder and louder, the humming sound of the bees throbbing against the hive. This horrible condition continued until the clock struck seven—and after that I don't remember anything more, since I lost consciousness.

This was the greatest good fortune that could befall me in my present, disastrous condition. I don't know if at this time I rested physically, but at least I didn't have to suffer imagining what awaited me, and what in reality, in its horror, would far surpass all the imaginings of my disturbed fantasy.

Chapter Eight

When I came to my senses the swarm of bees had flown off, and I found myself at the bottom of a deep, snowy pit. I lay at the very bottom with outstretched arms and legs and felt nothing, neither cold, nor hunger, nor thirst—absolutely nothing! Only my head was so cloudy and befuddled that it was really difficult to bring myself to remember what had happened and in what condition I now found myself. But finally all of this cleared, and the first thought that occurred to me at the time was that my guide came to himself before me, and sneaked out and left me.

Looking at it objectively, he should have done just that, especially after I threatened to baptize him yesterday and find his brother, Kozmo-Demi; but he, though a pagan, acted differently. As I, moving my swollen extremities with difficulty, sat up in the bottom of my open grave, I saw him about thirty paces from me. He stood under a great tree covered with hoar frost making quite curious movements; and in front of him on a long branch hung a dog, from its slit belly its warm entrails slowly poured down.

I figured out that he was making a sacrifice, or in their language a *tailga*, and it's true to say I wasn't upset that this animal sacrifice had kept him here until I could awaken and stop him from leaving me. But I was absolutely certain this pagan must definitely have such unchristian intentions, and was envious of Father Kiriak who at least was now suffering his misfortune with a baptized person who should be more trustworthy than my non-Christian. Could it be, maybe because of my difficult situation, that a suspicion was born in me—Father Kiriak, who foresaw better than I all the misfortunes which could happen in traveling in Siberia, under the cloak of kindness, might have fooled me and pushed this pagan on me, and

took for himself a Christian? Of course this wasn't like Father
Kiriak, and even now when I think of it I'm ashamed of my
suspicions; but what is one to do when they appear?

I got out of the snowy pit and started to walk toward my
native. He heard the snow crunch under my feet, turned around,
but immediately resumed his previous sacrificial ministrations.

"Well, don't you think you've bowed enough?" I said standing beside him for a minute.

"Enough, Fodder." And immediately he went to the sled and
started to put the harnesses on the dogs. When the outfit was
ready we started again.

"To whom did you give the *tailga*?" I asked him, motioning
back with my head.

"I don't know, Fodder."

"But to whom did you sacrifice the doggy, to God or to the
shaitan?"

"Shaitan, Fodder, of course—shaitan."

"What did you treat him for?"

"Because he didn't freeze us. I gave him a doggy for that.
Let him gobble it up."

"Hm! Yes, let him gobble it up. Isn't much to gobble, but
it's a pity about the doggy."

"Why's it a pity, Fodder? Doggy wasn't good, would die
soon anyway. It's all right, Fodder. Let him take it—gobble it."

"Yes, that's how you reckon it. You gave him a dying
one...."

"Of course, Fodder."

"But tell me, please. Where are we going?"

"Don't know, Fodder. We're looking for some tracks."

"Where's my priest-friend?"

"Don't know, Fodder."

"How can we find him?"

"Don't know, Fodder."

"Perhaps he froze?"

"Why would he freeze, Fodder. The snow here—won't
freeze."

I reminded myself again that Kiriak still had with him the
bottle with the warming drink and the provisions, and—felt

better. I had none of this, but now gladly would eat some of the dogs' dried fish, but was afraid to ask about it because I wasn't certain that we had any with us.

The whole day we drove around to no purpose. I could see it—if not by the expressionless face of my driver, then by the restless, uneven, nervous movements of his dogs, jumpy and continually moving from side to side. My native had a lot of trouble with them, but his unchanging, passionless, even-temperedness didn't leave him for a minute. He was merely working with his stick paying a bit more attention, without which attention, of course, on this day we would have been thrown out of the sled one hundred times and left either in the middle of the steppes or someplace by the forest we were passing.

But suddenly one of the doggies stuck its muzzle into the snow, jerked its hind legs and dropped. The native, of course, knew better than I what that meant, what new misfortune was threatening us, but didn't show any fear or confusion. Just as always, with a firm and steady hand, he stuck his stick into the snow and gave this anchor of our salvation to me to hold; but he himself quickly got off the sled, took the exhausted dog out of the harness and dragged it behind the sled. I thought that he wanted to finish it off and throw it away; but looking back I saw that the dog was already hanging in a tree and from it the bloody entrails again poured down. A disgusting sight!

"What's that again?" I shouted to him.

"It's for the shaitan, Fodder."

"Well, brother, that's enough for your shaitan. It's too much for him to eat two dogs a day."

"That's all right, Fodder, let him gobble."

"No, it's not all right," I said. "If you're going to butcher them like that, then you'll slaughter them all for the shaitan."

"I give him those that are dying, Fodder."

"It would be better if you fed them."

"There's nothing, Fodder."

"So that's it!" This was exactly what I was afraid of.

The short day again closed toward evening and it was evident that the rest of the dogs were quite tired, their strength left them and they began to cough wildly and to sit down. And suddenly one more fell down while all the rest, seemingly by agreement, immediately sat down on their tails and started howling, as though conducting a memorial service for it.

The native got up and wanted to hang the third dog for the shaitan, but this time I positively forbade it. I couldn't stand to look at it any longer, and it seemed as if this abomination was somehow increasing the horror of our situation.

"Leave it," I said, "and don't dare touch it. Let it die as it would."

He didn't argue, but with his usual, imperturbable calmness did the most unexpected thing. He quietly stuck his stick in front of the sled, and one-by-one unharnessed all the doggies and let them go. The hungry dogs seemed to forget their weariness. They yelped, gave a hollow bark, and the whole pack took off in one direction, and in a minute they were lost to sight in the woods beyond the fallow land in the distance. All this happened so fast, as the story about Ilya Murometz is told: "When he mounted the horse, everyone saw it, but how he left, no one saw." Our locomotion had left us; we *could leave by foot.* Of the ten not so long ago frisky doggies, only the dead one was left with us, lying by our feet in its harness. My native stood over this shameful scene leaning on his stick, and looked at his feet with the same passionlessness.

"Why did you do it?" I exclaimed.

"Let them go, Fodder."

"I see that you let them go; but would they come back?"

"No, Fodder, they won't come. They'll get wild."

"Why then, why did you let them go?"

"They want to gobble, Fodder. Let them catch a wild animal. They'll gobble."

"But what will we gobble?"

"Nothing, Fodder."

"Oh, you monster of cruelty."

He probably didn't understand and did not answer anything, but pushed his stick into the snow and started walking. No one could guess where and why he walked away from me. I called out, asked him to come back, but he only glanced at me with his expressionless look and growled, "Shut up, Fodder," and made his way farther along. Soon he disappeared into the skirts of the forest and I remained quite alone.

Is it necessary for me to go into detail about how terrible my situation was or maybe you will understand better the entire horror from the fact that I didn't think about anything except my hunger, that I didn't want to eat in the normal sense of the human desire for nourishment, but to devour food like a ravenous wolf. I got out my watch, pressed the button and was startled by a new surprise. My watch stopped—which had never happened before when it was wound. With shaking hands I put the key into the watch and came to the realization that it stopped because it had completely unwound; and it would run for forty-eight hours on one winding. This led me to believe that we were sleeping under the snow, lying in our icy grave, *more than twenty-four hours*! How long? Maybe two, maybe three days? Then I wasn't surprised I was suffering so much from hunger...That means it was the third day I hadn't eaten, and realizing this, I felt pains of hunger even more fiercely.

Eat, anything to eat!—dirty, foul, only to eat! That's all I could understand, desperately looking around with eyes full of unbearable suffering.

Chapter Nine

I was standing on a flat elevation. Behind me was a vast, boundless steppe, and in front it continued endlessly. On the right were marked depressions covered with snow which fell away, far beyond that on the horizon was the blue line of the forest where our dogs had disappeared. On the left were the skirts of another forest we were traveling along until our entire harness of dogs was released. I stood alone by the big snow bank which apparently had blown over a small hillock, covered with tall pines and firs that seemed to stretch up to the sky. Suffering from hunger, sitting on the edge of the sled, I was getting colder, not paying attention to anything around me, and I didn't notice when my guide appeared beside me. I saw neither how he came nor how he settled quietly beside me. Now as I paid attention to him, he sat with the driver's stick between his knees, while his hands were within his warm fur coat. Not a line of his face showed expression, not a muscle moved, and his eyes didn't show anything besides dull, calm submission.

I glanced at him and didn't ask him anything, while he, who till now never spoke first, maintained his silence. So we sat as twilight descended, and so we continued through the unending dark night, not saying a word to one another.

But at the first gray light, the native quietly got off the sled, pushed his hands deeper into his bosom, and again made his way along the outer line of trees of the forest. He didn't come back for a long time, and I watched him for a long time walking and stopping. He would stop and stare at the trees for a long, long time and then go on again. And finally he disappeared out of sight; and then again just as quietly and expressionlessly returned, and straightway climbed under the sled and began to arrange or disarrange something there.

metamorphosis

"What are you doing there?" I asked. And with this I unpleasantly discovered that my voice got lower, or even completely changed, but my guide spoke as before, then as now, words squeezed through his teeth.

"I'm getting skis, Fodder."

"Skis!" I exclaimed in horror. Only now did I completely understand what it meant "to sharpen skis."[1] "Why are you getting skis?"

"I'm running away right now."

"Oh, you villain," I thought; but said, "Where are you running to?"

"I'll run to the right side, Fodder."

"Why are you running there?"

"I'm bringing you something to gobble."

"You're lying," I said. "You want to leave me here."

But he didn't react to it at all and answered, "No, I'll bring you something to gobble."

"Where would you get me something to gobble?"

"Don't know, Fodder."

"How can you not know. Where are you running?"

"To the right side."

"Who's there on the right side?"

"Don't know, Fodder."

"If you don't know, then why are you running there?"

"I found a sign—there's a tent." "You're lying, my dear fellow," I said. "You want to leave me here alone."

"No, I'll bring to gobble."

"Well, go. Only it's better not to lie; but go wherever you want."

"Why lie, Fodder, it's bad to lie."

"Very bad, brother, but you are lying."

"No, Fodder, I'm not lying! Come with me. I'll show you the sign."

And grabbing hold of the skis and the stick, he dragged them behind him, and taking me by the hand, he brought me to a particular tree and asked, "Do you see, Fodder?"

1 An expression in Russian meaning "to run off."

"See what?" I said. "I see the tree, nothing else."

"There, in the great branched fork, twig upon twig, do you see it?"

"Well, so what? I see the twig. Probably the wind blew it there."

"What kind of wind, Fodder. That's not the wind, but a good person put it there. In that direction there's a tent."

Well, it's obvious that either he's trying to fool me or he's fooling himself; but what could I do? I couldn't hold him by force, and why should I hold him? Does it make any difference if I die alone or if the two of us die together from hunger and cold? Let him run and try to save himself, if he can be saved, and I told him as the monks do, "Save yourself, brother!"

But he quietly answered, "Thank you, Fodder," and with this he got up on his skis, laid the stick on his shoulders, pushed off with one foot, then again, and started skiing. In a minute he couldn't be seen, and I was left completely alone in the midst of snow, cold, and quite exhausted, suffering from starvation.

Chapter Ten

I spent the short Siberian winter day walking about the sled, sitting down and getting up again whenever the cold got worse than the unbearable tortures of hunger. Understandably, I was moving slowly because I didn't have any strength. Besides, if you move too fast, you get even colder.

Wandering near the place where my guide abandoned me, I frequently came to that tree on which he showed me the twig-sign. I examined it carefully and was even more certain that this twig was simply thrown there by the wind from another tree. "Deceived," I said to myself, "he deceived me; but let it not be counted as a sin against him. Why should he have to perish together with me, would it have done me any good?"

Is it necessary to describe to you how difficult and unbearably long this brief day seemed to me? I didn't believe in any possibility of salvation and waited for death; but where was it? Why did it delay and when would it decide to come? How long would I still have to suffer before it would embrace me and put my sufferings to rest?...I soon began to notice that at times my sight was impaired. Suddenly all the objects blended together and disappeared into some kind of gray haze, but then they would again suddenly, unexpectedly go clear...It seemed that this happened simply from fatigue, but I didn't know what role the changing light played here. When the illumination changed a little, everything became visible again, visible and very clear far into the distance, but then misty again. For an hour the sun popped out from behind the distant hillocks and poured a wonderful pure pink light over these same snow-covered hillocks. That happens there before evening, after which the sun goes down very fast and the pink light changes to the most exquisite blue. It was so now. Around me nearby everything got blue, as if covered by sapphire dust—wherever there was an indentation, wherever a footprint or simply a hole in the snow made by a stick. All over the bluish smoke was rising, and after a short time of this play of light everything got dark. The steppe was as if covered by an overturned chalice and then again it eased up...and became gray...With that last change, with the disappearance of this wonderful blue light, momentary darkness prevailed, different amazing tricks of the steppe began to appear before my tired eyes in the gray haze. All the objects began to have unbelievably huge proportions and outlines. Our sled stuck out like the hull of a ship. The frost-covered, dead dog seemed like a sleeping white bear, and the trees as if they came to life and started moving from place to place...And all of this was so alive and interesting that I, in spite of my unfortunate predicament, would have been willing to observe it with curiosity—if not for one strange occurrence which frightened me away from my observations and awakened a new fear in me, arousing with it the instinct of self-preservation. Before my eyes in the distance, in the half-darkness, something flashed for a moment like a dark arrow, then another, then a third, after which the air was pierced by a prolonged, mournful howl.

I instantly realized this was either wolves or the freed dogs which probably couldn't find anything edible and were unable to catch an animal; but quite exhausted from hunger, they had remembered their dead friend and wanted to make use of its cadaver. In any case, one or the other, hungry dogs or wolves, they wouldn't give any special consideration to "My Reverence," and although according to reason it would be easier to be torn apart right away than to starve to death, nonetheless the instinct of self-preservation took over. And with speed and agility—which to tell the truth I never knew I possessed and never expected—in my heavy clothes I climbed to the very top of the tree like a squirrel, and only then came to my senses when it was impossible to go any higher. In front of me spread out a whole expanse of snow, and reddish, dull stars blushed out of the distant, opaque darkness in a sky like thick foam. And while I took in this scene surrounding me, below just about at the base of my tree was some kind of scuffle, sounds of tearing, groaning, again struggling, and again groaning; and then again in the darkness the arrows flashed in all different directions, and immediately everything quieted down, just as though nothing ever happened. The scene became undisturbedly silent, so that I could hear my own heartbeat and breathing—which made a sound like the rustling of hay; and if you took a deep breath it seemed as if an electric spark quietly crackled in the unbearable, rarified, frosty air, so dry and so cold that even the hairs of my beard were frozen through, and pricked like wire and broke to the touch. Even now I feel a shiver as I remember, a memory forced on me by my frostbitten feet. Possibly it was warmer below, but maybe not; though in any case I didn't believe that the invasion of beasts wouldn't be repeated, and decided not to get down from the tree until morning. This wasn't any more terrible than digging in under the snow with my stinking comrade, and on the whole what could be more terrible than the entirety of my present circumstance? I merely chose the biggest fork between two large branches and settled in as into a comfortable chair, so that even if I did fall asleep I wouldn't fall down; and besides, for greater safety I put my arms around one branch and tucked them into my coat. My position was well-chosen and well-situated: I was sitting like a frozen, old owl, which by appearance I probably resembled. My watch had long since stopped, but from here I had a wonderful view of Orion and the Pleiades—those heavenly clocks, by which I could calculate the time of my suffering. That's what I was doing. First I calculated the approximate time, then simply without any purpose I looked for a long, long while at the unusual stars in the absolutely black sky until they started to fade. They changed from gold to copper, and finally got quite dim and went out.

Morning came, just as gray and joyless. My watch, set according to the Pleiades, showed nine o'clock. Hunger embittered everything and tormented me incredibly. I didn't experience any smell of food or remember any taste of it, but I just had a hungry pain. My empty stomach twisted and turned like a rope and caused me unbearable suffering.

Without any hope of finding anything edible I came down from the tree and began to wander around. In one place I found a pine cone in the snow. My first thought was perhaps it was a cedar cone and maybe it had a nut in it, but it turned out to be simply a common pine cone. I broke it, got the seed out and swallowed it, but the smell of tar was so unpleasant that even my empty stomach wouldn't accept it, and from it my pain only increased. At that time I noticed a great number of fresh tracks in all directions from our deserted sled and that our dead dog was gone. After this it would probably be my own dead body's turn, on which would descend the same wolves, and just as quickly and wildly they would divide it between themselves. Only when would this happen? Could it be another twenty-four hours? What if even longer?...No. I called to mind one religious fanatic who starved himself to death for the glory of Christ. He had the courage to count the days of his anguish and counted nine...That's terrible! But he did his starving in warmth, though I underwent the same in the most severe cold. That of course can make a big difference. My strength completely left me. I couldn't any longer get warm by moving around and sat down on the sled. Even consciousness of my fate seemed to have left me. I felt the shadow of death on my eyelids and only regretted that it led me so slowly on the path of no return. You understand how earnestly I wanted to go away from this frozen steppe to the assembled home of all mortals, and had no regrets that here in this cold darkness I would make my bed. The chain of my thoughts broke down, the jug was broken and the wheel over the well collapsed: no thoughts, not an appeal to heaven in the most familiar form. Nothing, nowhere, no way could be gotten. I understood that and sighed.

Abba Father! I can't even give You my repentance, but You Yourself have moved my light from its place, so You must answer for me before You!

That was all the prayer I could collect in my mind, and then I remember nothing, how the day proceeded. All the same, I can say with certainty that it was exactly like the previous one. It just seemed to me that on this day I saw in the distance two living things, and they seemed to be two birds of some kind. They seemed to me to be the size of magpies and in appearance similar to magpies, but with badly dissheveled feathers which looked like an owl's. Right before sunset, they flew from somewhere in the trees to the snow, walked around and flew away. But, perhaps, it only seemed so to me in my dying hallucinations; however, it looked so clear that I watched their flight and could see how they disappeared in the distance, as if they melted. My tired eyes, getting to this point stayed there, and were fixed. But what do you think? All of a sudden I noticed in that direction a strange dot, which it seemed wasn't there before. Also it looked as if it were moving, though it was so imperceptible, with movements you could feel more than see with your eyes; but I was positive that it was moving.

Hope for salvation was reawakened, and all my sufferings weren't strong enough to drown it out and stifle it. The dot was growing, all the time clearer, and it became even clearer on the wonderful pale pink background. Is it a mirage, so possible in this deserted place with its capricious illumination, or is it really something alive hurrying towards me; but in any case it flies straight at me, and really does not walk but flies. I see how *it* draws toward me in a straight line, at last I can see a figure— see its feet. I see how they shuffle one after the other...following this I quickly change my joy back to despair. Yes, this is no mirage—I see it very clearly, but it's also neither human nor beast. Actually, there is no such embodiment on earth which would look like this magical, fantastic sight, which approaches me, as if it were condensing, forming, or as the spiritualists now say, "materializing," out of the playful shades of the frozen atmosphere. Or are my eyes or my imagination deceiving me?—or whatever you say, but it's a spirit. What kind? Who are you? Possibly my Father Kiriak is hurrying to meet me from the kingdom of the dead...But could it be that we are already both *there*?...Could it be that I already finished my crossing? How nice! How curious this spirit, my new fellow citizen in the new life! I'll describe him to you as I can: A winged, gigantic figure swam toward me clothed from head to toe in a chiton of silver brocade, sparkling all over. On its head a huge headpiece which seemed seven feet tall was afire and looked as if it was all covered with diamonds, or more precisely a diamond-covered mitre...All of it was similar to a richly-dressed Indian idol, and to crown the likeness to the idol and its fantastic appearance, from under the feet of this marvelous guest showered sparks of silver dust, by which it seemed to float on a light cloud, at the very least like the legendary Hermes.

And so, while I was looking at it, he, the wondrous spirit, continually came closer, closer, and—at last quite close, and in one more moment, sprayed all of me with snow dust, pushed in front of me with his magic wand and exclaimed, "Hello, Fodder!"

I couldn't believe my eyes or ears. This wondrous spirit was, of course, he—my native! Now there could be no further mistake. Here under his feet were the same skis on which he left, on his back another pair, in front of me pushed into the snow his stick, and in his arms the whole haunch of a bear, complete with fur and the clawed paw. But in what was he dressed, into what had he been transfigured?

Not waiting for any kind of answer on my part to his greeting, he pushed the bear meat in my face, and bellowed, "Gobble, Fodder!" He himself sat down on the sled and started to take off his skis.

Native as salvation

Chapter Eleven

I grabbed hold of the ham and chewed and sucked the raw meat, trying to relieve the hunger tormenting me, and at the same time watched my deliverer.

What was it that was on his head, that kept it all in the same magical, shining, great headpiece? I could no way grasp what it was and said, "Listen, what's that on your head?"

"That's," he answered, "that you didn't give me money."

I must admit, I didn't quite understand what he wanted to say to me with this; but looking at him more intently, I discovered that the high, diamond headpiece was nothing other than his own long hair. All of it was entirely permeated with snow dust, and as it flew when he ran so it froze, looking like shocks of wheat.

"Where's your fur hat?"

"Left it."

"Why?"

"Because you didn't give me money."

"Well," I said, "I really did forget to give you money, that was stupid of me; but what kind of unfeeling person was your host that he didn't believe you and took your hat in such cold."

"Nobody took my hat from me."

"Then what happened?"

"I left it myself." And he described to me how he was skiing and following the track the whole day, found the yurt—a bear lay in the yurt—but the owner wasn't home.

"Well?"

"Thought that if you'd wait long, Fodder, you'd croak."

"Well?"

"I chopped the bear and took a paw and skied back, but left him my hat."

"What for?"

"So that he wouldn't think bad, Fodder."

"But this owner doesn't know you."

"This one doesn't know, Fodder, but the other does."

"What other?"

"That Owner Who's watching from above."

"Hm! The One that watches from above?..."

"Yes, Fodder, what else: He sees everything, Fodder."

"He does, my brother, He does."

"What else, Fodder. He doesn't like those who do bad things, Fodder."

The deliberation was very close to that used by Saint Sirin when seduced by a temptress who invited him into her house, but he invited her to sin in front of everybody in the square. She said, "You can't do that there. *The people will see it*." But he said, "I wouldn't pay much attention to people, but what if God sees us? We'd better go our own ways."

"Well, brother," I thought to myself, "it seems that you're not far from the Kingdom of Heaven." But during my short thought he plopped down in the snow.

"Excuse, Fodder," he said, "you gobble but I want to sleep." And he began to snore in his mighty manner.

It was already dark. The black sky again stretched over us where rayless stars shone like sparks on tar.

I had already eaten a little by then, that is, swallowed a few small pieces of raw meat, and stood with a piece of bear meat in my hands over the sleeping guide and asked myself, "What is the enigmatic journey this pure, noble spirit is making in this clumsy body in this horrible wilderness? Why is he embodied here and not in a country blessed by nature? Why is his mental capacity so meagre that it couldn't reveal the Creator to him in more extensive and clearer concepts? Why, O God, was he deprived of the possibility of thanking You for his enlightenment by the light of Your Gospel? Why doesn't my hand have the means to regenerate him to a new, glorious birth into Your sonship by Your Christ. Your will should prevail over everything. If You, in his sad existence, illumine him with the divine light from above, then I believe that this light of his understanding is a gift from You! My Master, how am I to comprehend? What should I do not to anger You and also not to offend him?"

While in this meditation I didn't notice how the sky suddenly blazed up, caught fire, and poured a mysterious light over us. Everything took on huge, fantastic proportions and my sleeping deliverer appeared to me enchanted, a mighty, legendary hero. I bent over him and started to look him over, as if I never saw him before, and what am I to tell you? —He looked beautiful to me. It seemed to me he was: the one whose neck bore the yoke of power; the one whose mortal foot trod the way, whom wild birds knew not; the one before whom terror fled, who reduced me to weakness, caught me in the noose of my own connivance. Poor is his speech, and by the movement of his lips he couldn't console a sorrowing heart; but his word—this is a spark in the movement of his heart. How eloquent is his virtue, and who could bring himself to grieve him?... In any case not I. No, as the Lord lives, grieving him for the sake of my soul, that I wouldn't do. Let my shoulder fall off my back and my arm break away from my elbow if I raise my hand against this poor soul and his poor kind! Forgive me, blessed Augustine, if now and again my opinion differs from yours, and I don't agree with you now that apparently, "the very virtues of pagans are only hidden vices." No. The one who saved my life did it for nothing except virtue, by his selfless compassion and nobility. He, not knowing the precept of the Apostle Peter, "took courage for me (his adversary), and committed his soul to works of charity." He left his fur hat and skied twenty-four hours in his icy cap, of course, moved not only by a *natural* feeling of compassion for me, but also having *religio*, cherishing *union* with the Owner "Who looks from above." What am I going to do with him now? Would I take from him this religion and break it, when I have no possibility of giving him another better and sweeter, since "the words confuse a mortal's reason"; and it's impossible to demonstrate anything to captivate him? Could I use fear to force him, or seduce him by benefit of protection? Never would he be like Hamor and Shechem, who let themselves be circumcised for the gain of Jacob's daughters and cattle![1] Those who try to gain cattle and daughters by faith will gain not faith,

1 Genesis 34.

but only cattle and daughters, and an oblation from their hands
would be to You as if it were swine's blood.[2] But where are my
means to educate him, to *enlighten* him, when there are none of
these means, and everything seems to have been specifically
arranged so that I couldn't have them in my hands? No, probably my Kiriak was right. There is a seal here you cannot break
with the unliberated hand—and a welcome thought came to me
in the counsel of the Prophet Habakkuk: "Though it tarry, wait
for it; because it will surely come, it will not tarry."[3] Yea, come
Christ, yea, come Yourself into this pure heart, to this kind soul;
for while You are slow, for while You aren't to do it now... let
the snowy hillocks of his fields be dear to him, let him end his
days shedding life as the vine yields its ripened fruit, as the wild
olive its bloom... It's not for me to put a shackle on his feet and
persecute his ways, when He Who Is[4] wrote the commandment
of love in his heart with His finger and has led him away from
deeds of anger. Abba Father, make Yourself known to him who
loves You, not to him who questions; and may You be blessed
to the ages—to me and to him and to everyone—to each whom
You allow by Your goodness to comprehend Your will. There
is no more trepidation in my heart: I believe that You revealed
Yourself to him according to his need, and he knows You as
everything knows You:

> Largior hic campos aether et lumine vestit
> Purpureo, solemque suum, sua sidera norunt![5]

These ancient words of Virgil came to me, and I bowed my head to
the earth near the head of my native; and getting on my knees, I blessed
him and covered his frozen head with the skirt of my coat, and slept
by him as I would sleep embracing the angel of the wilderness.

2 Isaiah 66:3. The blood of swine carries a double proscription, since each
   (blood and swine) is separately a forbidden food in the Old Testament.
3 Habakkuk 2:3.
4 The term, "He Who Is," is the Church Slavic equivalent to the Old Testament
   name of God, Yahweh. (Originally in Hebrew the word was most probably a
   verbal form used as the name, and was thus translated in Greek and Church
   Slavic.)
5 Here an ampler ether clothes the meads with roseate light,
   And they know their own sun, and stars of their own. (*Aeneid*, Book VI.
   640).

Chapter Twelve

S hould I tell you the end? It's not more complicated than the beginning.

When we woke up, the native fitted me with the skis he brought with him, cut down a stick for me, put it in my hands and taught me how to hold it; then he put a rope around my waist, took the end of it and pulled me behind him.

You ask, Where? First to pay the debt for the bear meat. There we hoped to get some dogs and go farther; but we didn't go where my inexperienced venture was taking me at the beginning. In the smoky yurt of our creditor one more lesson awaited me, which had a very definite significance for all my following undertakings. The matter was such that the owner for whom my guide left his hat was not hunting at the time when my deliverer arrived, but he was rescuing my Kiriak after his Christian guide abandoned him in the midst of the wilderness.

Yes, gentlemen, in this yurt near a dim, stinking fire I found my noble elder, and in what a horrible, heart-rending condition! He was all frozen. They smeared him with something, and he was still alive, but a horrible smell overpowered me when I drew close to him, telling me that the spirit watching over his abode was about to depart. I picked up the reindeer skin that covered him and was horrified. Gangrene separated all the flesh on his legs from the bone, but he could see and talk. Recognizing me he whispered, "Hello, Your Grace."

In indescribable horror I looked at him and couldn't find the words.

"I was waiting for you and you came. Thank God. Did you see the steppe? How did it look to you?...Never mind, as you live, you will gain experience."

"Forgive me, Father Kiriak," I said, "for leading you here."

"Enough, Your Grace. Blessed be your coming here. You received experience and live, but confess me quickly."

"Good," I said, "right away. Where did you put the Holy Gifts? Weren't they with you?"

"They were with me," he said, "but now they're not."

"Where are they?"

"The native ate them."

"What are you saying?"

"Yes!...He ate them! Well, what's there to say?—an ignorant fellow...a confused mind...Couldn't stop him...He said, 'I'll meet the priest. He'll forgive me.' What's there to say?...He mixed up everything...."

"Is it possible," I said, "that he ate the Chrism?"

"He ate everything, even ate the sponge, and took the Communion set with him, and left me...He believed that 'the priest will forgive'...What's there to say? —a confused mind...Let's forgive him this, Your Grace. May Christ only forgive us. Give me your word you won't look for him, the poor fellow, or...if you do find him..."

"Then forgive him?"

"Yes. Forgive him for Christ's sake and...when you get home, see that you don't tell the little enemies anything about him; because they, those evil ones, might show their zeal over that poor fellow. Please, don't say anything."

I gave my word, and getting on my knees by the dying man, started to confess him; and at the same time a parti-colored shamaness jumped into the yurt full of people and started to beat her tambourine; and others followed her on wooden, tuned forks, and still others on some kind of unknown instrument, of the time when tribes and peoples 'fell down before the image on the plain of Dura at the sound of the cornet and all kinds of musick.'[1] And so started a wild ceremony.

This prayer was for us and for our deliverance, when it might have been better for them to pray for their deliverance

1 The Church Slavic paraphrase, here translated into a paraphrase of the King James Bible, is a reference to the scene in the Book of Daniel, chapter 3, wherein Babylonian music is played on various instruments before idol worship takes place.

from us. And I, a bishop, was present during this prayer. And Father Kiriak was giving up his spirit to God, and either he was praying or arguing with Him like the Prophet Jeremiah, or negotiating like a true evangelical swineherd, not with words but with wordless sighs.

"Have mercy," he whispered. "Make me now as one of Thy hired servants![2] The hour has come...return me to my former image and inheritance...don't let me be an evil devil in Hades; drown my sins in the blood of Jesus, send me to Him!...I would like to be dust at His feet...Declare: 'So be it'..."

He took a breath and again called, "O goodness...O simplicity...O love!...O my joy!...Jesus!...Now I run to Thee like Nicodemus at night; hasten to help me, open the door...let me hear God, walking and speaking!...Now...Thy garment is already in my hands...break my thigh[3]...but I won't let Thee go...until Thou blessest everyone with me."

I love this *Russian* prayer, how in the twelfth century it flowed from our Goldenmouthed Kirill of Turov and which he willed to us: "Pray not only for your own but for others, not only the Christians, but for those of other beliefs, so that they can turn to God." My dear elder Kiriak was praying like that. *For everyone* he dared: "Bless *everyone*," he said, "or I won't let Thee go!" What can you do with such a character?

With these words he stretched himself out—as if he were dragged by Christ's garment—and flew away...Even till now it looks to me as if he's still holding on, hanging on, carried behind Him and pleading: "Bless *everyone, or I won't let Thee go.*" The daring old man will probably beg his way; and That One by His goodness will not refuse him. With us in the *family* of Christ all this is done *in sancta simplicitate.*[4] Whether we understand Him or not we may discuss as you wish, but that we live with Him simply—this really seems indisputable. And He simply loves....

---

2 Luke 15:19.
3 Of the many Church Slavic expressions that dot Father Kiriak's speech, this one refers to the story of Jacob wrestling with God (Genesis 32). The earlier reference to Nicodemus comes from the Gospel of John (chapter 3).
4 Latin, "in blessed simplicity."

Chapter Thirteen

I buried Kiriak under a mound of earth on the shore of a frozen stream, and at the same time learned from the natives the revolting news that my successful Zyryan baptized...I'm ashamed to say, with *refreshment*—or simply put, with vodka. In my eyes this whole business seemed so covered with shame that I didn't want to see or hear about this baptizer, but returned to the city with a resolve to sit in my monastery at my books— without which there's deadly destruction to a monk with idle thoughts—and in between times to tonsure ordinands quietly, and reconcile readers and their wives. But as to holy work, which in holiness can never be performed carelessly, it's better not to start at all: "Don't offer folly to God." That's what I did, returned to the monastery—now grown wise with the experience that my long-suffering missionaries were good people, and thanked God they were that and not otherwise.

Now I saw clearly that honest weakness is more excusable than mindless zeal—in that matter where there is no way to apply mindful zeal. Of such impossibility, I was convinced by papers which awaited me at the monastery in which it was communicated "For Your Information" that in Siberia, besides the 580 Buddhist lamas on the assigned staffs of thirty-four temples, there are also lamas that are unattached. So what? I'm not a Koniushkevich or an Arsenii Matsievich. I am the bishop of a new school and I don't want to sit in Reval[1] with a gag in my mouth as Arsenii sat, and besides it doesn't change anything...I accepted the news of the increase in lamas sent "For Your Information," and as fast as I possibly could recalled my Zyryan from the steppes, and awarded him a *nabedrennik*[2]—

1 The city called Reval by Europeans, known to nineteenth-century Russians as Revel', is better known now as Tallinn in Estonia. The medieval Russian name for the city was Kolyvan'.

like a spiritual sword—for his success, and kept him in the town at the cathedral as vestment-keeper and supervisor of the regilding of the iconostasis.[3] And I gathered my leisure-bound missionaries, and bowed low to them and said, "Forgive me, fathers and brothers, for I did not understand your goodness."

"God forgives," they said.

"Well, thank you for being merciful, and from now on and always above all be merciful, and the God of mercy will be present in your works."

And from that time through all the rest of my sufficiently long stay in Siberia I was never perturbed, even if the quiet work of my preachers did not give the efficacious results desired by the impatient religious circles of high society. When there were no such effects I was at peace that "the water jars were filled one at a time"; but when all of a sudden one or another of the missionaries appeared with some big numbers...frankly, I must tell you that I felt anxious...I would remember either my Zyryan...or one of the Guard, Ushakov, who baptized, or the Councilor Iartsev, both were even more wonderfully, hastily successful, for with them as in the days of Vladimir, "piety was mediated with fear," and the unbelievers, even before the arrival of the missionaries, already begged baptism from them...And what came out of all their eagerness and "piety mediated with fear"? The abomination of desolation was produced in the holy places, where the fonts of these eager baptizers were, and...in that, everything became confused—the mind, the heart, and the people's understanding; and I, a bad bishop, was unable to do anything about it, but even a good one couldn't do anything, until...until, so to say, we seriously occupy ourselves with faith, not pluming ourselves for the looks of it like the Pharisees. So, gentlemen, we Russian baptizers find ourselves in such a situation—not that we don't understand Christ, but really because we understand Him and don't want

2 An initial award for priests of the Russian Church signified by a one and one-half foot square of cloth worn at the side and below the belt with full vestments.

3 An "iconostasis," "iconostas," or "icon screen" is a partition with doors and (usually, tiers of) icons that separates the sanctuary from the nave in Orthodox churches.

His name to be used in vain among the heathen. And so I lived, not by my former precipitous despotism, but patiently, and even perhaps lazily, bearing the crosses—from Christ and not from Christ—which fell to me. The most interesting of which was that I had zealously begun to study Buddhism; and I by my Zyryan's report was reputed to be a secret Buddhist...So it remained with me, although I didn't stop the zealousness of my Zyryan and allowed him to act according to the well-tested and successful methods of Prince Andrei Bogoliubskii, which were exclaimed over Andrei's casket by Kuz'ma, one of his household: "When a heathen comes, you command him to be brought to the sacristy. *Let him look at our true Christianity.*" I let the Zyryan bring in whomever he wanted, to enter the sacristy and thoroughly show everything of "true Christianity" collected there by our people and him. All this was good and effective enough. They approved of our "true Christianity," but still my Zyryan no doubt was bored to baptize people by twos and threes, and it really was boring. Now I have uttered a genuine Russian word, "boring"! At that time, gentlemen, it was boring to struggle with the self-satisfied ignorance that tolerated faith only as a political means; but now it might be even more boring to struggle with the indifference of those who, instead of enlightening others, "themselves hardly believe," to use the apt phrase of the before mentioned Matsievich. But you contemporary intellectuals all think, "Oh, our diocesan bishops are no good! What are they doing? Our bishops, they do nothing." I don't want to defend everybody. Many of us really have become very feeble, stumbling beneath our crosses, falling down. And it's not just anyone—but the big-time operators and more than one *popa mitratus*[4] who has become some kind of bishop for their sake. And all this, to be sure, works on the principle of "What will ye give me?"[5] But I would ask you, What brought them to this point? Isn't it simply that they, your diocesan bishops, have been turned into administrators and now can do *nothing* vital? And you know, perhaps you owe them a great debt of gratitude that they do nothing at this time. Otherwise, they might have strapped you

---

4 Latin, "a mitered priest."
5 The Church Slavic quotation cited from Matthew 26:15 begins the episode of Judas's betrayal of Jesus for thirty pieces of silver.

with such an unbearable burden that, God knows, either your spines would have shattered into smithereens or the strap would have snapped in half. But we bishops are *conservative*. We preserve, insofar as we can, the "liberty wherewith Christ hath made us free"[6] from such "assistance..." So gentlemen, that's why we operate and cooperate poorly. Don't thrust in our faces the example of former hierarchs like Saint Gurii and others. Saint Gurii knew how to enlighten—it's true. And this is why he went to that savage country well-outfitted: with the order and power "to attract the people with kindness, with food-stuffs, *with defense* against state officials, *with the right of appeal* for grievances before regional chiefs and judges." He "*was obliged to*" take part in government councils. But our present-day bishop isn't even allowed to confer on business with his neighboring bishop. It's as if he mustn't think about anything. He has someone to think for him, so he's only obliged to accept all of it sent "*For Your Information.*" What do you want from him, if even now he has nowhere to appeal for himself?...O Lord, may Thy will be done...What can be done is somehow done by itself, and I saw this at the end of my pastorate in Siberia. Once a missionary came to me and said that he had happened upon a nomad encampment at the place where I buried my Kiriak, and there by the stream he baptized a whole crowd to the "God of Kiriak," just as people were once baptized in the name of the "God of Justin." A good people by the bones of the good elder learned to love and understand the God Who made this good soul, and they themselves wanted to serve God, Who brought into existence such spiritual "beauty."

For this I ordered a massive oak cross to be placed over Kiriak's grave, which would not even be renounced by the Galician Prince Vladimirko, who thought kissing a small cross had no force. We erected a cross to Kiriak twice as tall as the Zyryan. And that was the last order of my Siberian pastorate.

I don't know who might chop down this cross, or might have already chopped it down—Buddhist lamas or Russian officials. And in any case it makes no difference....

So this my tale to you is finished. Judge all of us by what you see. I won't justify myself, but I'll tell you one thing, my

6 Galatians 5:1.

simple Kiriak certainly understood Christ no less than those
imported preachers of ours, who are sounding cymbals in your
living rooms and your winter gardens. There they should remain, among the wives of Lot, of whom not one, whatever
words she might hear, will leave for Zoar; but she will make
pretense before God—while our life here in Russia is a bit too
boring—and with the littlest change in her life, she'll look back
again at Sodom and change into a pillar of salt.[7] That's what all
the success of drawing-room, mock-Christianity will consist of.
What to do with these miracle-workers? They don't want to
walk on the bottom but to fly at the top. But since they're like
locusts, with small wings and great bodies, they'll not fly far,
nor will they shed the light of faith or the sweetness of consolation on the fogs of our native land, where from woodland to
woodland walks *our* Christ. Our Christ is blessed and kind, and,
above all, so patient that even the very least of His servants He
teaches to watch submissively those who destroy His work,
which is being destroyed by those who especially should be
most afraid of doing so. We've gotten accustomed to everything
because it's not the first snow that has fallen on our heads.
There was a time they used to hide our *Rock of Faith*, but
pushed the German-made *Hammer*[8] into everybody's hands,
and they wanted to cut our hair and shave us, and change us into
little abbés.[9] One benefactor, Golitsyn, was telling us to preach
his foolish theology. Another, Protasov, was shaking his finger
threateningly under our very noses. And a third, Chebyshev,
even surpassed all of them, and at the bazaar, as in the Synod,
openly spewed forth "putrid words," convincing everyone that
"there is no God and to speak about Him is stupid"...But whom
will we suddenly come upon next, and what new rooster or

7 The reference is to Genesis 19.

8 The *Rock of Faith* was a polemical work written against Protestant influ-
   ences in Russia by the temporary administrator of the patriarchate, Metropolitan Stefan (Iavorskii), during the reign of Peter I—who had great
   sympathy with German Lutheranism (and also successfully abolished the
   patriarchate completely during Iavorskii's tenure). The *Hammer*, with the
   nuance "the Sledge to the Rock," a work of unknown authorship, was the
   reply.

9 The word might be translated "abbots," but has the nuance in Russian of
   an intrusive, foreign term, because it is not the usual ecclesiastical word
   for the head of a monastery.

other will crow to us, you can't even guess. One consolation is that all of them, these activists of the Russian Church, couldn't do anything to Her, because it's an unequal fight. The Church is indestructible as the apostolic edifice, but the spirit of these cockerels will pass and they'll not have come to know their own place. But what I find extremely tactless, gentlemen, is this: Some of these highly placed personages, widely stationed as they are now called, don't notice our modesty and don't value it. This, to tell the truth, is ingratitude: They don't have reason to reproach us for being patient and kind...If we were a little more impatient, God knows whether many wouldn't regret it, and most of all those who toil not and who receive not the wounds among men, but grown fat on their thighs, idly philosophize about what they should begin to believe in order to have something to philosophize about. Gentlemen, at least appreciate the holy modesty of Orthodoxy and understand that it faithfully holds to the spirit of Christ, if it suffers *all* which it pleases God to suffer. Truly, its humility alone is worthy of praise; but one must marvel at its vitality[10] and glorify God for it.

Without prompting we all involuntarily answered, "Amen."

10 The word in Russian may mean "vitality" or "tenacity."

Notes

Translator's Preface

p. 17 *A note on non-Christian religions*

Although precise information regarding the nature religions or the forms of paganism of these different native peoples cannot be given here, some characteristics of nature religion in general might be helpful for those unfamiliar with the phenomenon. First of all, the world view of non-urban pagan societies was dependent largely on nature. In them it was common to find the elemental forces of nature—wind, water, earth, thunder, frost, sun, moon, etc.—personified, or even deified, and interacting with human society or particular human beings. Similarly, animals were frequently found with voice and rationality in folk tales, imparting the wisdom of their ways to humankind. Since all these forces were thought to control crop growth, vital to agricultural peoples, and fecundity and availability of game, vital to herdsmen and hunters, knowing and respecting them appeared necessary for human survival. Sacrifice fit mechanically into the perceived cause and effect of those forces in daily life. The calendar, which marks such things as the times of rainfall, fertility of crops and animals, and the movement of herds, was associated with astrology, and took on the same central significance of sustaining life.

On the human side of the equation, two social institutions complemented nature religion. The first was the tribal, gens religion, sometimes called the cult of the ancestors. The second was the development of a priestly class of society. In the first social institution one finds such phenomena as the cult of the clan and the cult of the dead. Both emphasize kinship associations and the importance of tribal and familial membership. Through this institution one learned the value of the group for survival, the respect of persons, the knowledge of tradition—a living, communal experience—and so forth.

The second institution provided human society with applied knowledge as well as the religious functions of priestcraft. Members of this caste might be called shaman, druid, sorcerer, wizard, magician, etc. All knowledge was doubtless considered esoteric by everyone involved, so that understanding the calendar, treating people medically, and advising people on the properties of herbs were placed on the same level as forecasting the future, casting spells, and training villains: all had religious connotations. The shaman was given the status of a gnostic, one who knew or one who was a "keeper of secrets." He was to remember and repeat the archaic spells. Sometimes he also performed a religious role in tribal leadership.

Unlike missionaries in the West who were often given to minimizing or disparaging the paganism of native groups, the Eastern Church since the time of Clement of Alexandria (second century) has taken a different tack. Thus, these religions—including the nature religions—were not to be off-handedly condemned or even disregarded. They were to be considered a necessary preparation for the proclamation of the Gospel to the peoples. This approach produced both positive and negative results. The most significant positive consequence was that indigenous cultures were not destroyed by assimilation; but they were gradually transformed into bearers of the Christian tradition, insofar as Christianity over time could show itself to be legitimately superior to the "old ways." The obvious negative consequence was that the "old ways" might well continue unabated for centuries, with idolatry and superstition consuming human resources and retarding cultural development.

Chapter One

p. 23   *"The guests were all intellectuals and an interesting conversation
         began among them on our faith and faithlessness [or unfaith]"*
One might surmise that Leskov is setting the stage with an appropriate quote from J. W. Goethe—a bench mark for nineteenth-century European intellectuals—in the back of his mind: "The profoundest, nay, the one theme of the history of the universe and of mankind, the theme to which all others are subordinated is the conflict between faith and unfaith."

p. 23f. *"Your Eminence"*
A direct form of address for bishops, *Vladyko* in Russian, equivalent to *Despota* in Greek, is literally translated "Master"; but since this appellation is not used in English, it has been rendered "Your Grace" for a bishop and "Your Eminence" for an archbishop.

p. 24   *"Tübingen, London, or Geneva"*
These cities represent the European theological centers of the Lutheran, Anglican, and Reformed Churches, respectively.

p. 24   *"he took from the table a large album, richly decorated with
         carved ivory"*
In addition to a lively interest in pilgrimages to the Holy Land, archaeology, and Bible translation, many educated Russians of the nineteenth century, like other European Christians, enjoyed viewing large pictorial albums of Biblical scenes painted by the world's great artists, for example, *The Bible in Paintings of Famous Masters* (Saint Petersburg: A.S. Suvorin, 1901, in Russian).

p. 24 *"Here He sits by the well with the Samaritan woman—a wonderful work."*

Though this gospel scene from John 4:4 was recreated by many artists, the picture referred to here is probably Rembrandt's "Christ and the Samaritan" from 1655. When Rembrandt repainted the scene in 1658 Christ's countenance was more severe toward the woman.

p. 24 *"Christ here is kissed by Judas"*

The portrait referred to here is probably Reubens's "Kiss of Judas" which Leskov called "a portrait of genius by a genius, Reubens."

p. 25 *"Titian"*

Titian (1477?-1576) painted the portrait "Caesar's Denarius" which hangs in Dresden.

p. 25 *"the sculptor Cauer"*

The German sculptor Robert Cauer (1831-1893), or Robert the Elder, worked on the "Head of Christ" from 1862-1869 for the Church of Saint Paul in Shwerin, east of Hamburg. Robert's father, Emil Cauer (1800-1867), laid claim to fame as a sculptor in Germany, not only with his works and teaching, but with the invention of a substitute for plaster, known as the "Cauersche Masse." Robert's brother, Karl Cauer (1828-1885), was also a student of his father, an accomplished artist in his own right, and is known to Americans for his design of President Garfield's tomb in Cleveland. Five of the two brothers' sons also became sculptors.

p. 25 *"what a horrible countenance Metsu has given Him!"*

Gabriel Metsu (1629-1667) was a Dutch artist, but the portrait about which Leskov speaks is probably that of an earlier Flemish artist, Quentin Metsys (1465/6-1530) or (usually) Massys of the Antwerp school ["The Crucifixion"(?), Ottawa, Canada].

p. 25 *"Lafond, perhaps not a great artist"*

The French artist Alexandre Lafond (1815-1901) painted the portrait "Christ in the Grotto" in 1861 which fits Leskov's description.

p. 26 *"the 'Sacré coeur' which the Jesuit fathers preach"*

Devotion to the "Sacred Heart," characterized by feelings of passion and sentimentalism, grew up especially in France in the seventeenth century and was propagated by the Jesuit Order, among others.

p. 26 *"This lady—the Lord strengthen her—first explained to me the secret of how to find Christ" [emphasis added]*

A case can be made for Leskov attacking Lord Radstock through a few non-specific allusions. (See also p. 114.) Lord Radstock, Granville Augustus William Waldegrave (1833-1913), variously referred to by Russians as Radstock, "Redstock," and "Krestok" (little cross), preached evangelical sermons with great success in private homes in Saint

Petersburg's high society. As one observer noted, "Not to be a Radstock-ist meant to lower oneself in the eyes of society and risk the danger of becoming labelled a backward person. To take exception with the teaching of the English Lord in a private home was considered equal to insulting the host." See Leskov's 1877 book, *A High-Society Schism* (*Velikosvetskii Raskol*).

After finishing Oxford with honors, Lord Radstock devoted himself to evangelism and Christian philanthropy. His preaching tours took him to France, Holland, Switzerland, India, and three times to Russia: 1874, 1875-1876, and 1878. It was most especially on his protracted trips to Russia that he gained fame there. As a religious figure, he probably should be classed in the evangelical circles that included D. L. Moody in the U.S., with whom he wrote *Gospel Dialogues*, and with Dr. F. W. Baedeker in Russia, for whose biography he wrote an "introductory note." By the time of his third trip to Russia he no longer preached in broken French to the Saint Petersburg elite, but in his own acquired Russian. As an example of the proceedings of a prayer meeting, the following selection is offered. (Note the emphasis below on the objective, "to find Christ," which Leskov has already incorporated satirically in the first chapter.)

"Lord Radstock's appearance in aristocratic society had at first an atmosphere of strangeness about it; an English peer, an equal to his listeners, in simple house dress, a layman who propagated the word of God as a Christian and yet adhered to no specific denomination, was indeed a unique phenomenon at this time in St. Petersburg. His services were of the simplest kind, almost a repetition of those held in France and in Switzerland. First, a silent prayer before his audience was offered for divine guidance. This would be followed by the reading and explanation of certain passages from the Bible lasting an hour. His commentaries were never prepared, thus there were numerous repetitions and frequent shifts of thought. In spite of this he never lost his main objective, the presentation of the fundamentals of the Gospel, the belief in salvation through the atoning death of Jesus Christ, and the assurance that salvation was open to all who desired it. The meetings were dispersed after a prayer and a hymn and, above all, after an invitation to those who wished 'to find Christ' to call upon Lord Radstock at a later date. All this was executed in a conversational tone, almost in a whisper without emotion or eloquence, but with a deep conviction" (Edmund Heier, *Religious Schism in the Russian Aristocracy 1860-1900: Radstockism and Pashkovism* [The Hague: Martinus Nijhoff, 1970], pp. 44-45).

p. 26   *"the secret of how to find Christ"*

The root of the Russian word translated "secret" may also mean "mystery" or "sacrament" (compare the Greek, *mysterion*). Whenever these

English words appear in translation, usually the same root is present in Russian.

p. 26 *"I would readily prefer this Jewish-looking head by Guercino"*

The Italian artist Giovanni-Francesco Barbieri (1591-1666), "Il Guercino" or "The Squinting One," painted "The Crown of Thorns" which hangs in Munich and which Leskov had in mind.

p. 26 *"according to the formulation of Mr. Renan"*

(Joseph-)Ernest Renan (1823-1892) was a French historian of religion, semiticist, and philosopher whose chief work was the multivolumed *Histoire des origines du christianisme* (1863-1883, *History of the Origins of Christianity*). He was appointed professor of Hebrew at the Collège de France in 1862, soon dismissed, but reinstated in 1870. His dismissal was a result of his teachings on the person of Jesus, which appeared in print in the famous *Vie de Jésus* (1863, *Life of Jesus*) as the first volume of his history, cited above. He also maintained a special interest in science (E.g., *L'Avenir de la science*: "Science is a religion... science alone is able to solve all problems and will someday displace religion.") and messianism. He was very influential in Europe in the 1870's.

p. 26 *"turn your eyes to the icon corner which is directly behind you"*

In every Russian Orthodox home one expects to find an icon corner, if indeed there is not one in every room. The icon there, frequently of Jesus Christ, is displayed in the eastern corner of the room at an elevation higher than that of any other wall decoration. Daily prayers, prayers before meals, etc. are said before the icon. For information on icons accompanied by color illustrations, see L. Ouspensky and V. Lossky, *The Meaning of Icons*, 1989.

One should keep in mind that at the time Leskov was writing Russian culture ran after western portraiture as superior to traditional iconography. People frequently replaced icons—even in churches—with portraiture at the expense of the canon of traditional iconography, not to mention the important spiritual dimension of the medium. Leskov's veiled reference—the listeners have their backs to the icon while the archbishop has been facing it all the while—should not go unnoticed.

p. 27 *"according to the system of Lavater"*

Johann Kaspar Lavater (1741-1801) was a famous Protestant minister who led an anti-rationalist religious movement in Switzerland. He is remembered primarily for his foundational work in "physiognomy," a pseudo-science which described the art of analyzing the (divine!) character of a person by his outward appearance. Lavater's four volumes were read extensively throughout Europe.

p. 27   *"from Petersburg to Kamchatka"*
These locales represent the farthest reaches of the great landmass of the
Russian Empire, the city of Saint Petersburg in the west on the Gulf of
Finland and the Kamchatka peninsula in the east on the Bering Sea—sep-
arated by a distance of over 4,000 miles.

Chapter Two

p. 29   *"I was still a fairly young man and was consecrated bishop and
assigned to a very remote Siberian diocese"*
Bishop Nil was transferred from Vyatka to Irkutsk, Siberia, in 1838,
where he remained as bishop until 1854.

p. 29   *"I ordered a number of eagle rugs"*
In this section we briefly embark on some intricacies of the Russo-Byz-
antine liturgy. The eagle rug is a small, round rug about a foot and
one-half in diameter with the representation of an eagle hovering over the
bishop's see or city of residence. The bishop stands on such a rug during
the religious services. Since the bishop moves to various places during
the Divine Liturgy—the center of the church, in front of the altar, behind
the altar, etc.—the placing of the eagle rugs when they are in short supply
becomes a distraction from, rather than an addition to, the solemnity of
the service.

p. 30   *"I restrained the deacons from grabbing me by the elbows during
the liturgical services and also from perching next to me at the
high place, but most of all from cuffing and squeezing the backs
or the necks of the poor ordinands"*
Due to the advanced age of many hierarchs, and the cumbersome quality
of some episcopal vestments, it is common for the deacons to support the
bishop by the elbows when he moves from place to place during the divine
services. When the deacons forget that a particular bishop is young, the
presumed help becomes a hindrance.

The high place, located behind the altar in the most eastern part of
the apse (and sometimes including a raised platform and a bishop's
throne), is reserved solely for the bishop who represents Jesus Christ.
Deacons, especially protodeacons, are occasionally infamous for liturgical theatrics; and, at times, they forget the spiritual significance of their
office and prefer to occupy "center stage." This phenomenon explains
both their perching on the edge of the high place and the rude behavior
displayed to the advancing ordinands—whom they are supposed to help
lead through the ordination. Here, instead, they are making the process as
painful as possible.

p. 30   *"in those olden days"*
The expression is Church Slavic, used to introduce a liturgical Gospel
reading (equivalent to the Latin, *in illo tempore,* and rendered in English

by "at that time" or "in those days"), and is for the Russian reader a recognized archaism.

p. 30   *"Squint-eyed, lame, nasal-toned, fools, and even... some possessed."*

A category of saint possibly alluded to here, "the fool in Christ" (in Russian, *iurodivyi vo Xriste*), has been a controversial one over the centuries. At times the Church has questioned whether to recognize it, although recently the Russian Church canonized Xenia of Saint Petersburg, numbered in this group. The basis of the controversy regarding "holy fools"—which partially explains Leskov's reference—may be summarized to say (possibly, too simply) that the saints could not easily be distinguished from the retarded, the demented, and others. Thus, the term "holy fool" frequently had, and still has, a slightly pejorative connotation. In *Travel Notes* Bishop Nil ushers forth a whole series of examples of Siberian church employees who are total illiterates, spiritually infirm, and economically destitute. He writes: "And these especially, Yakut and Tungus and even Russians, must study the principles of the faith and Christian morals. But should we wait for success there, where the blind lead the blind?" (p. 225) [For more information see the chapter "The Holy Fools" in G. P. Fedotov, *The Russian Religious Mind*, Vol. II (Cambridge, Mass.: Harvard University Press, 1966.)]

p. 30   *" 'Come let us worship God, our King' "*

The prayer,

> "Come let us worship God, our King,
> Come let us worship and fall down before Christ,
> our King and our God,
> Come let us worship and fall down before Christ Himself,
> our King and our God,"

begins many of the liturgical services, especially the daily services, morning and evening.

p. 30-31 *" 'Thou who at all times and at every hour in heaven' ... 'hallowed be Thy Name, Thy Kingdom come.' "*

The reader is jumping from the beginning of a familiar prayer used in the Hours to the beginning line of the Lord's Prayer, "in heaven, hallowed be Thy Name...." The English text of the first prayer may be found in Isabel Hapgood, trans., *Service Book of the Holy Orthodox-Catholic Apostolic Church* (Englewood, NJ: Antiochian Orthodox Christian Archdiocese, 1975), p. 47.

p. 31   *"finished the evening prayers... O Holy Trinity—my compliments to You' "*

The text of the prayer of Saint Ioannikios is familiar to the Russian Orthodox church-goer:

The Father is my hope,
The Son is my refuge,
The Holy Spirit is my protection,
O Holy Trinity, glory to Thee!

p. 31   *"It was necessary to try to find an inspector..."*
By this point the archbishop has become the main narrator and will
continue as such, almost uninterrupted, until the last line of the story.

p. 32   *"generously treated himself to some homemade liqueur; and this,*
         like many others made from local wild berries, produced...intox-
         ication"
The term for "homemade liqueur," literally *oblepixa*, a type of berry, is a
Siberian dialectical word referring to a sloe liqueur. The "local wild
berries" are probably Siberian black currants.

Chapter Three

p. 35   *"Not only nomads adhered to the 'dual-faith'"*
The term "dual-faith" or "two beliefs" is a familiar one to the Russian
reader, since it is used to describe the popular religion of old Rus' after
the conversion of Vladimir, when Christianity and paganism existed side
by side—and joined together—among the common folk.

p. 35   *"Yakut" (and Tungus languages)*
See the Translator's Preface.

p. 36   *"placed the Chrism and Holy Communion kits on the altar"*
    Both Chrism, the oil for anointing the newly baptized, and Holy
Communion are carried in special receptacles over the heart, hung from
the neck by a chain or ribbon. When not in use they are kept in a
tabernacle on the altar. [The Latin names for the receptacles are
chrismatorium and pyx(is) or ciborium.]

p. 37   *"Good day, Your Grace"*
The bishop and monk always speak using the familiar "you" (second
person singular), similar to "thou" in English.

p. 39   *"he, not having his own altar, literally lives off his priest's*
         traveling sacramentary kit"
With the reduction of church support from the imperial government after
the "Spiritual Regulation" of Peter the Great, it became common for
clergy to live off (in part) donations paid for private services. These
"needs" or *treby* originally referred to religious services for the needs of
individuals, i.e., special prayers. The term—because of the deplorable
living conditions of the priests—began to be identified with the monetary
needs of the clergy, just to live. (The contrast between the connotation of

the term "honorarium" and that of the term "needs" speaks for itself.) The system is still widespread in the Russian Church today.

p. 41 *"Simple it is, Your Grace, like the Trinity itself in its unity—simple existence"*

The line is a paraphrase from the lenten "Canon of Saint Andrew of Crete," a popular, lengthy, penitential service celebrated during Great Lent in preparation for Pascha (Easter).

p. 42 *"The moral: I didn't know, being foolish, what I asked for, but nevertheless my wish was granted so that I would learn a lesson."*

This moral, or literally "the meaning" in Russian, is one which Kiriak learned as a child, but it has been left for others in the story—and possibly the reader—to learn as adults. Since it recurs in the pages to come, it might be considered a leitmotif.

p. 42 *"We thrice exchanged the kiss of peace"*

The kiss of peace, in this circumstance, is a sign of spontaneous joy, since it would have been customary for the monk simply to receive the bishop's blessing and leave.

Chapter Four

p. 43 *"the venerable Gurii"*

Of the three saints named Gurii (equivalent to Gurias, Gurian) commemorated in the Russian church calendar, the holy man under consideration is not the fourth century Syrian martyr mentioned in the Roman Martyrology (November 15 in both the West and Russia), but the first archbishop of Kazan, of the noble family Rugotin, remembered on December 5th. A monk of the Volokolamsk Monastery, Gurii was made archbishop of newly conquered Kazan by Tsar Ivan (IV) the Terrible in 1555. Here, over the course of nine years, he converted many thousands of Moslems and pagans to Christianity through preaching and the instruction of children. He taught the children to read; and he was such a zealous preacher that when sick, they would carry him to church on a stretcher and he would instruct his flock from there. During the last two years of his life he devoted himself to asceticism, died in 1595, and was buried in the Transfiguration of the Savior Monastery. He is especially venerated in the Kazan region.

p. 44 *"the Chronicles"*

Although various Chronicles—annals or year by year records of events— were known from different areas of ancient Rus', the one referred to here is called the *Primary Chronicle* or the *Tale of Bygone Years*. A monk of the Kiev Monastery of the Caves, known now as Nestor the Chronicler, was one of the final redactors of this history, beginning with the evolution of the Kievan state in the ninth century. The editing was done in the eleventh century. A translation is available in English, entitled *The Russian Primary Chronicle*, by S.H. Cross and O. B. Sherbowitz-Wetzor. For expert information on the Chronicles in general, consult Fedotov, *Religious Mind*, pp. 265-314.

Leskov here refers to the baptism of Rus' under Prince Vladimir, dated to 988, which is one of the hallmark events of this chronicle. In the not too distant past the Chronicles were read as "straight history," while more recently their intentionality has been closely examined and they have been found to have a historiographical agenda. For example, some historians would now say that Vladimir prematurely coerced the Kievan population into a mass baptism in the Dnieper—a position quite different from the triumphalist description in the Chronicles. Kiriak seems to hold the more modern opinion.

p. 44 *"Metropolitan Platon"*

Platon Levshin (1737-1812) was one of the remarkable churchmen of the eighteenth and early nineteenth centuries. Brought to Saint Petersburg in 1763 as preacher to the court of Catherine (II) the Great, he advanced initially on his preaching abilities—over 500 of his sermons are preserved. He was also tutor to the Grand Duke Paul. Recognized as the greatest educator of the church schools of the eighteenth century, he worked to improve not only the Latin curriculum of the clergy but their cultural, social, and material status in Russia. Affected by the spirit of the Enlightenment, he wrote both the first systematized theology and outline of church history in Russian, and strove to bring theology into contact with life, largely through catechesis. In his thirty-seven year tenure as Metropolitan of Moscow, his successful administrative abilities brought much of his vision to fruition.

p. 44 *"Thus, we're baptized into Christ, but don't clothe ourselves in Christ."*

Kiriak's language depends upon the theology of Saint Paul, "For as many of you as were baptized into Christ have put on [or clothed yourselves in] Christ" (Gal. 3:27). This line is used as a hymn in the Orthodox Church during the baptismal liturgy and is familiar to the average parishioner. Leskov's views regarding baptism expressed here—the necessity of instruction, the dangers of ritualism devoid of content, etc.—are also found in his 1872 novel, *Cathedral Folk*, "The Unbaptized Priest" (1877), and again in "Episcopal Justice" (1877) and in "Jewish Somersault" (1882). The last two instances both relate to the "Jewish question," and more particularly to baptism as an element in the Russification of Jewish boys forcibly conscripted under Tsar Nicholas I.

p. 44   *"Saint Cyril of Jerusalem on the baptismal mysteries: 'Simon the*
         Magician [or Simon Magus] wet his body with water in the font,
         but his heart was not illumined by the Spirit, his body went down
         into the water and came up, but his soul was not buried together
         with Christ, nor with Him raised'"

The difficult Church Slavic passage Leskov cites is from "The Pro-
catechesis," 2, of Saint Cyril's (d. 386) work on baptism. See *St. Cyril of
Jerusalem: On the Sacraments*, 1977, p. 1 and pp. 40-41 for the full text
of the Greek original and an English translation.

p. 47   *"at the completion of all my lessons...like a graduating student—*
         to Kiriak's cell."

The relationship between student and teacher in prerevolutionary Russia
was much different from that in the West today. Once the frequent
corporal punishments of the early grades were passed by, education at the
advanced levels was very personal and represented a permanent debt the
disciple owed the instructor. The grades the students received were considered to be a reflection on the educator, to a certain degree, rather than
purely an indicator of learning performance. Professors and teachers were
usually poor and depended on pupils for sustenance. For their entire lives
students were expected to remember the sacrifice their mentors had made
in order to provide them with an education. Students frequently brought
sustenance and gifts to their teachersf as a form of "social security."

Chapter Five

p. 50   *"this kind cannot be exorcised, neither by prayer nor fasting"*

The quote is a clever reversal of the saying of Jesus, "This kind never
comes out (or is exorcised) except by prayer and fasting" (Mt. 17:21). In
the story Jesus cast a demon from a boy when his disciples could not. [The
verse is not included in many modern English language Bibles—it is in
the King James Version— because it is not attested by all ancient authorities.]

p. 50   *"Lives of the Saints"*

Both in original composition and in translation, a great deal of the
literature of ancient Rus' was devoted to lives of saints. For example,
within one hundred years of the death of Boris and Gleb, sons of Prince
Vladimir, in the early eleventh century three different hagiographies (that
is, lives of saints) were written about the brothers. Nestor the Chronicler
wrote a *Life* of Theodosius of the Kievan Caves Monastery within twenty
years of his death—ten years before he was canonized—as well as other
lives he included in the Chronicle. The lives of Palestinian saints and the
Syrian *Historia Religiosa* of Theodoret of Cyrrhus were two models of
ascetic life for Kievan Christianity, and certainly must have been some of
the earliest material translated from Greek. The later style of Russian

hagiography was established in the fifteenth century by Epiphanius the Wise and Pachomius the Serb. In the nineteenth century the standard collection of *Lives* consisted of twelve thick volumes, one for each month, compiled by Saint Dmitri of Rostov (d. 1709) during the latter twenty years of his life.

p. 51   *"Reason brings forth doubts, Your Grace, but faith gives peace, it gives joy..."*

Here Kiriak is repeating an old axiom of the Eastern Fathers, that faith has the ability to apprehend truth—and God to a certain extent—when *ratio rationalis* fails human experience. For example, it is written in *The Cloud of Unknowing* of God, "He may well be loved, but not thought. By love can He be caught and held, but by thinking never." The Fathers' perspective is not so much a condemnation of human rationality (or Western rationalism) as it is an affirmation of both the transcendence and the immanence of God and the mysteriological content (i.e. "sacramental," in the wider sense) of the complete human experience—of which rationality comprises only a part.

p. 52   *"It's as if we've been given a ticket to a banquet."*

Kiriak's comparison is traditional since the image of a messianic banquet was popular in first century Palestine, and also was used by Jesus in parables and miracles to refer to the Kingdom of God. The image was later incorporated into the literature of Kievan Rus' through the portrait of the idealized Christian prince, the prince who provided food in abundance to all his subjects. Paramount among these were the feasts of Prince Vladimir, who even sent carts laden with food through the city for those physically impaired from attending. Entertainment provided by the prince was included in the proceedings of the banquets as well, provision of which was elevated to the status of a Christian virtue in Russia—ergo, the beginnings of Russian hospitality.

p. 55   *"Kiriak," I said, "too many books are making you mad."*

The young bishop does not appreciate being upbraided with a quote from Revelation by the older hieromonk, and retaliates with an allusion to Acts 26:24—Paul's classic defense of Christianity before King Agrippa. His choice of texts is ironic and unfortunate, for he has adopted the speech of the Roman provincial governor, Festus, in attacking Saint Paul. Likewise, Kiriak in reply mirrors Paul's response, "I am not mad, ...but I am speaking the sober truth."

Leskov has intentionally interpolated the scene from Acts so that Kiriak will make the same reply as did Paul to Festus, thus drawing a parallel between Kiriak and Paul. (See the note above for p. 44 which also relates Kiriak and Paul.) With this wonderful repartee the author has not only established the relative spiritual authority and condition of his two main characters, but has encouraged the identification of Kiriak with the first

"Apostle to the Gentiles" (Paul) and the bishop with a somewhat sympathetic, but unwitting, party to his co-conversationist's execution (Festus).

p. 55   *"not only simple-hearted Amos of the Old Testament, who used to gather berries, suddenly began to prophesy"*

The reference to Amos as a gatherer of berries is comparable to the description of the prophet in the King James Version of the Bible as "a gatherer of sycomore fruit" (Amos 7:14). [N.B. The reading used in this particular instance by Leskov's Russian Bible and the KJV is dependent on the Greek Septuagint rather than on the Hebrew, which in either case is perplexing and open to speculation.]

p. 58   *"By this time my neighbor, the bishop, had already served out his term"*

The word "term" in Russian, *epitimia*, is used to mean repentance or ecclesiastical punishment; but it is actually a Greek word having the above meaning and additional meanings, one of which is public service. If Leskov had the double entendre in mind, the play would be between serving out a term of public service as bishop and serving out a term of punishment in remote Siberia.

p. 59   *"Lake Baikal"*

The largest freshwater lake in Asia (the Caspian is a salt water lake), Lake Baikal is located in southern Siberia just north of the center of Mongolia, with the city of Irkutsk on its southern shore. The deepest lake in the world (5,710 ft.), it has a surface area of over 13,000 square miles.

Chapter Six

p. 64   *"...or else they would surpass Kirik himself with questions..."*

A group of Novgorodian priests addressed 101 questions to Bishop Nifont in the mid-twelfth century, one of three similar documents we have from the period. Known as the *Questions of Kirik* (since his name headed the list of priests), the queries may be characterized as legalistic, and focus on a ritualistic understanding of the faith.

p. 64   *"Is it possible to commune someone who taps his teeth with an egg?"*

In order to understand the complexity—and absurdity—of this question one would have to appreciate three unrelated, yet plausible, items:

1. Indeed, a person might be found tapping his teeth with an egg. A popular game exists among Slavs in which boiled eggs—usually colored Easter eggs—are struck against one another to see which one breaks. The winner eats the loser's egg. Aficionados of the game choose the hardest eggs by tapping them against their front teeth, sounding the shell for thickness and strength.

2. The fasting practice for Great Lent, a forty day period before Easter, prohibits the eating (or tapping?) of dairy products, including eggs.

3. The fast for Holy Communion prohibits the eating of any food from the time of the preceding evening.

[Angels on the head of a pin seem to be a bit more manageable.]

p. 69   *"Cosmas or Damian?"*
Cosmas and Damian were brothers and are commemorated in the Church catholic as "unmercenary physicians," that is, doctors who practiced medicine without demanding money. They are remembered as healers of humans and animals from a time late in the third century. Although immensely popular among the Byzantines and mentioned in both the western and eastern liturgies, their lives for the most part defy research— to such a degree that one has a choice among three or four sets of brothers by the same name who were unmercenary physicians from vastly different parts of the ancient world.

p. 73   *"Karl [von] Eckartshausen"*
Exceptionally popular in nineteenth-century Russia and unknown elsewhere, Karl von Eckartshausen (1752-1803) began his career in Bavaria as a jurist but soon turned to mysticism and alchemy. The popularity of his numerous writings, all of which had to be translated into Russian, may be credited to two circumstances: the first was preoccupation with mysticism among the elite dilettantes of the early nineteenth century, e.g., Tsar Alexander I, A. Golitsyn, R. Koshelev; and second was his personal acquaintance with I. V. Lopukhin, who first translated his writings. (Among other things, Lopukhin devoted himself to publishing mystics and freemasons at Moscow University.)

p. 74   *"Massillon or Bourdaloue"*
Both preachers to the court of Louis XIV, Jean-Baptiste Massillon (1663-1742) was a teacher and bishop in France, known as "the Racine of the pulpit," while Louis Bourdaloue (1632-1704) was a Jesuit whose preaching was considered exemplary, modeled upon classical homily. Their sermons were popular reading in nineteenth-century Saint Petersburg among those interested in homiletics, e.g., Metropolitan Filaret of Moscow.

Chapter Seven ———————

Chapter Eight

p. 86   *"as the story about Ilya Murometz is told"*
Like Sir Lancelot of King Arthur's round table, Ilya Murometz was the strongest and most courageous of the epic heroes (*bogatyr'*) surrounding Prince Vladimir. A representative of Christianity, Ilya—named for the prophet Elijah who ascended in a fiery chariot—sat debilitated on a bench

for thirty years, after which time he was healed. He then began to perform feats of valor, victories over characters who personified the wild southern horde.

p. 86 *"we could leave by foot"*

Here Leskov puns the word *opeshit'*, which is colloquial and means "to be taken aback, to be nonplussed, dumbfounded, amazed"; but instead, he gives it a folk etymology and makes it mean "to be reduced to foot locomotion." Special thanks to Professor McLean for this observation.

Chapter Nine

p. 90 *"there's a tent"*

The Russian word used for "tent" connotes one made of skins or bark. Elsewhere in the story Leskov uses a different Russian word of Turkic origin for "tent," "yurta" or "yurt"—both of which exist also in English.

Chapter Ten

p. 96 *"I called to mind one religious fanatic"*

This religious fanatic was a member of a Russian sect of Old Believers, literally *zaposhchevantsy*, who rejected the Christian priesthood. In general these priestless sects of Old Believers (*bezpopovtsy*) were like the ancient Montanists and Messalians. They also had a negative world view and believed their rites brought them into direct contact with the Holy Spirit, so that Christ could be reincarnated in various persons generation after generation. The sect Leskov refers to was characterized, in addition, by extreme asceticism and ritual suicide.

Chapter Eleven

p. 102 *"Saint Sirin"*

This saint is not listed in the calendar of the Russian Orthodox Church although a strong oral tradition attests to the story Leskov relates; but a similar, though not identical, life exists for the early fourth century martyr Serenus, who is commemorated in the West on February 23.

p. 104 *"an oblation"*

The roots that form the word for "an oblation" in Church Slavic are difficult and probably refer to a seven-fold gift. Thus, when the critical note to the Soviet edition of Leskov translates the word as a "fine white flour," it most likely connotes a flour sifted seven times, a flour fit to be a sacrificial cereal offering. In any case, the only mention of swine's blood in the Bible, Isaiah 66:3, is in relation to a cereal offering, and was doubtless the text Leskov had in mind.

p. 104   *"Here an ampler ether clothes..."*
In the footnote the English translation of the Latin is from H. Rushton Fairclough, trans., *Virgil*, Vol. I (Cambridge, Mass.: Harvard University Press, 1953), pp. 550-551.

Chapter Twelve

p. 107   *"And I, a bishop, was present during this prayer."*
One of the reasons the bishop emphasizes that he stayed through the dervish-like ceremony with musical accompaniment is because he was prohibited from doing so by Canon Law. He knows well that "No one shall join in prayers with heretics or schismatics" (Synod of Laodicea, Canon XXXIII)—let alone with heathens.

On occasion, Russian Orthodox churchmen have been fond of quoting this canon, even today, usually in an anti-ecumenical spirit. In point of fact the majority of nineteenth-century Russians only had rare opportunity to break the canon, other than with Old Believers—who constituted a special case. Most Russians of that era could have lived their entire lives without seeing anyone of another faith. A noted example of this is the priest John Popov-Veniaminov—better known as the sainted metropolitan of Moscow, Innocent—who commented that on a trip to California from Alaska, it was the first time in his life he had ever seen a Roman Catholic.

p. 107   *"Goldenmouthed Kirill of Turov"*
A premier orator, Bishop Kirill (1130-1189) or Cyril, gave rhetorical yet dynamic sermons which are preserved in a collection which follows the church's liturgical year (*Torzhestvennik*). Kirill employed classical Byzantine literary forms and theology in his sermons, letters, and prayers, as did his contemporaries. Stylistically he may be considered eclectic but lively. For more on Kirill, including short examples of his writing, see Fedotov, *Religious Mind*, pp. 69-83.

Chapter Thirteen

p. 109   *"Koniushkevich"*
During Leskov's day it was believed that Paul Koniushkevich (d. 1770) legitimately sought to propagate the Christian faith in Siberia when he was Metropolitan of Tobol'sk (c. 1758), but was slandered and retired to the Monastery of the Kievan Caves. Research late in the nineteenth century indicated that his removal from office was justified.

p. 109   *"Arsenii Matsievich"*
A notable instance of imperial persecution, the confinement of this metropolitan of Rostov (1697-1772) began after he anathematized Catherine (II) the Great for depriving the monasteries of their property rights (1763). He, in turn, was deprived of his metropolitanate, reduced to the rank of monk,

and cloistered in a monastery. Nevertheless, in the monastery he did not desist from railing against Catherine. After four years he was tried and convicted a second time, not as a cleric, but as a political prisoner under the name "Andrei Vral'"—which is not really a name, but means "Andrew the Liar." Following the second trial he was "shut up" in the prison in Reval, that is to say, not only was he physically incarcerated, but his mouth was gagged. According to the Canon Law of the Church—not to mention considerations of humane justice—both the trials and penalties were highly irregular.

p. 111   *"Prince Andrei Bogoliubskii"*
Grandson of Prince Vladimir Monomakh and a distinguished political figure of ancient Rus', Andrei (1110-1174) of Rostov and Suzdal was known for his many battles. In 1169 he sacked Kiev and moved the capital to Vladimir, also removing the beautiful Byzantine icon of the Mother of God with Child which subsequently has been known as Our Lady of Vladimir. The famous historiographical description "Caesar by his earthly nature is similar to any man, but by the power of his dignity he is similar to God alone," was first applied in Rus' to Andrei. In spite of continual contention with his bishop, he was canonized soon after [because of?] his violent political assassination on 29 June, the eve of the Feast of Saints Peter and Paul.

p. 111   *"I let the Zyryan bring in whomever he wanted, to enter the sacristy and thoroughly show everything of 'true Christianity' collected there by our people and him."*
The bishop, cleverly resourceful in his plan, knows the reason this display of aesthetics had to keep the Zyryan occupied and *quiet*. It was a well-known fact that the preceding quote from the eulogy of Prince Andrei Bogolubskii was used by Saint Stephen of Perm for missionary propagation in the fourteenth century—*to convert the Zyryans.*

p. 111   *"Isn't it simply that they, your diocesan bishops, have been turned into administrators and can now do* nothing *vital?"*
For a balanced, historical description of the genuine difficulties of the Russian Church hierarchy in the nineteenth century—*and their proposed and attempted solutions*—see James W. Cunningham, *A Vanquished Hope*, 1981. Cunningham confirms Nil's complaint.

p. 113   *"the 'God of Justin'"*
Justin Martyr (d. 165), also known as the Philosopher, was an apologist who first attempted to reconcile Christian belief with Greek philosophy. Of the many works attributed to him by the church historian Eusebius of Caesarea, only the *Apologies* against the pagans and the *Dialogue with the Jew Trypho* are extant today. Also of historical importance is *The Acts of Saint Justin and his Companions* which contains the official Roman court proceedings against Justin and six of his companions, all of whom were scourged and beheaded. One writing, possibly the lost *Confutation of the*

Greeks or a pseudo-Justinian work, seems to have been devoted to convincing a pagan by logical proof to accept Christianity as the faith "in the god whom Justin serves." Many theologians posit that the spread of Christianity in the early centuries occurred as a result of not only evangelism and teaching, but of Christian martyrdom. In fact in Greek, the word "martyr" also means "witness."

p. 113 *"the Galician Prince Vladimirko"*
Late in the 1140s Vladimirko was one of three princes competing for the dominance of Rus', including Izyaslav of Kiev (grandson of Vladimir Monomakh) and Yuri Dolgoruky of Suzdal'. Izyaslav was allied with Geza of Hungary, while Vladimirko maintained allegiance to the Byzantine Emperor Manuel Comnenus. Known for cunning and deceit, Vladimirko "kissed the cross," or swore an oath not to break an alliance with Izyaslav and Geza, but he quickly proceeded to betray them. When confronted by their ambassador, who pointed out to him that he had kissed the cross, Vladimirko rejoined, "What's a little cross to me!"

pp. 113-14 *"my simple Kiriak certainly understood Christ no less than those imported preachers of ours"*
Regarding "those imported preachers," see the note above for p. 26 referring to Lord Radstock.

p. 114 *"they wanted to cut our hair and shave us, and change us into little abbés"*
The reference is to the sweeping reforms of Peter the Great for the Russian church and clergy, actually written by Feofan Prokopovich and known as the "Spiritual Regulation." Many historians consider these reforms not only to have westernized, but also to have begun the secularization of, the church by the imperial government. Lest the western reader think that hair cutting and shaving are trivial matters, they are only outward symbols for far-reaching, devastating reforms that covered everything from Peter's abolition of the Russian patriarchate down to his prohibition against the monks' having pen and paper in their rooms.

p. 114 *"One benefactor, Golitsyn"*
A favorite of Tsar Alexander I, Prince Alexander N. Golitsyn (1773-1844) enjoyed a religious temperament characterized by extreme Biblicism and mysticism. These personality traits, peculiarly juxtaposed, probably would have been of little consequence had Golitsyn not been appointed Ober-Procurator of the Holy Synod, chief of the department of foreign confessions, Minister of Public Education, and elected president of the Russian Bible Society—among other offices. A genuine philanthropist and aristocrat, Golitsyn's tenure in affairs religious has been described as dictatorial and ruthless (G. Florovsky). He advocated his understanding of the Bible and mysticism by advancing like-minded obscurantists to official posts. His career in religious matters ended abruptly in 1824 due to charges of

insufficient Orthodoxy, although he remained head of the postal department and continued in the Council of Ministers and State Council.

p. 114 *"Another, Protasov"*
Count Nikolai A. Protasov (1799-1855) was Ober-Procurator of the Holy Synod from 1836 till the end of his life; and during that time he successfully transformed the church into an organ of the state, "The Department of the Orthodox Confession." As a retired cavalry officer he worked for the Ministry of Education and exercised tremendous influence over secular education, and later over the system of ecclesiastical schools. His viewpoint and style may be described briefly as that which attempted to reduce the church and the clergy to functionaries of civil religion in the worst sense—bureaucratic representatives of the state's "confession." With this as his goal, real higher education and ecclesiastical freedom became unnecessary. All that was necessary could be supplied by the tsar, who was "the supreme defender and guardian of the dogmas of the ruling faith, and observer of orthodoxy and all good order in the Holy Church." Under Protasov church monies and the employment of all clergy became the sole domain of the Ober-Procurator. Of those who opposed him, Metropolitan Filaret of Moscow distinguished himself by consistently attempting to keep Protasov in check.

p. 114 *"And a third, Chebyshev"*
P. P. Chebyshev, a retired brigadier, was Ober-Procurator of the Holy Synod from 1768-1774 under Empress Catherine.

pp.105-09 *A note on historical images*
Although the references on the last pages of the book are obscure to the average American or British reader—and therefore need to be explained—they are familiar and very powerful for Leskov's Russian audience, and constitute a fitting, emphatic conclusion.

N.B. Translations of other works of Nikolai Leskov exist in English (see McLean's book, mentioned in the Translator's Preface, for a complete listing of the fiction), although many stories remain available only in Russian. The reader who is seriously interested in Russia's past should see Nicholas V. Riasanovsky, *A History of Russia.* 4th ed. New York: Oxford University Press, 1984. [The fifth edition is to appear in 1993.] This is a readable history with an intelligent selection of materials. The theologian or specialist who enjoyed these notes might also enjoy *Ways of Russian Theology* by Father Georges Florovsky.